ICONS OF POWER

THE MAGIC IN HISTORY SERIES

FORBIDDEN RITES
A Necromancer's Manual of the Fifteenth Century
Richard Kieckhefer

CONJURING SPIRITS
Texts and Traditions of Medieval Ritual Magic
Claire Fanger

RITUAL MAGIC
Elizabeth M. Butler

THE FORTUNES OF FAUST
Elizabeth M. Butler

THE BATHHOUSE AT MIDNIGHT
An Historical Survey of Magic and Divination in Russia
W. F. Ryan

SPIRITUAL AND DEMONIC MAGIC
From Ficino to Campanella
D. P. Walker

ICONS OF POWER
Ritual Practices in Late Antiquity
Naomi Janowitz

The Magic in History series explores the role magic
and the occult have played in European culture, religion,
science, and politics. Titles in the series will bring the
resources of cultural, literary, and social history to bear on the
history of the magic arts, and will contribute towards an
understanding of why the theory and practice of magic have
elicited fascination at every level of European society.
Volumes will include both editions of important texts and
significant new research in the field.

MAGIC IN HISTORY

ICONS OF POWER

RITUAL PRACTICES IN LATE ANTIQUITY

NAOMI JANOWITZ

THE PENNSYLVANIA STATE UNIVERSITY PRESS
UNIVERSITY PARK, PENNSYLVANIA

Library of Congress Cataloging-in-Publication Data

Janowitz, Naomi.
Icons of power : ritual practices in late antiquity / Naomi Janowitz.
p.   cm. — (Magic in history)
Includes bibliographical references (p.   ) and index.
ISBN 0-271-02147-0
1. Magic, Jewish—History—To 1500.   2. Ritual—Rome.   3. Magic, Ancient.
I. Title. II. Series.
BF1622 .J45 2002
291.3'8'093—dc21   2002001255

For Andy

Contents

Acknowledgments

For general intellectual guidance, comments on individual chapters, and answers to specific technical questions, I want to thank Michael Silverstein, Richard Parmentier, Gregory Shaw, David Olster, Cale Johnson, Sara Rappe, and Rebecca Lesses. Editorial help came from Priscilla Stuckey, Devorah Schoenfeld, Jonathan Cale Harris, and Abby Limmer. Peggy Hoover at Penn State Press edited the manuscript with great care. Thanks are due to the series editor Richard Kieckhefer and to Peter J. Potter, editor-in-chief at Penn State Press. Chapter 2 was previously published in slightly different form in *Reflexive Language: Reported Speech and Metapragmatics,* edited by John Lucy, whose his meticulous work improved the chapter greatly. The chapter was also delivered as a paper at the Center for Psychosocial Studies in Chicago, Illinois, and the comments from the participants were very valuable. *History of Religions* published a version of Chapter 3. The research was supported by grants from the University of California–Davis.

Introduction

During the first centuries of the Common Era, Jews, Christians, and adherents of Greco-Roman religions engaged in a stunning and bewildering variety of rituals, and practitioners from these traditions deployed all manner of wonders. Individuals traveled through the heavens to see flaming chariots and hear angels give praise. Imprecations were used to summon angelic assistants to a host of tasks, including procuring lovers and evading enemies. Practitioners used knowledge of cosmic secrets and divine names in their rites and could also show their power by transforming metals, thus revealing the hidden processes of nature.

All the rituals depended on making an alliance with superhuman powers. Once manifested on earth, divine power could be used for everything from settling an old score to changing the very nature of earthly existence. Small tasks and major transformations were all enacted in the context of a finely calibrated cosmos where human speech and action were inextricably bound up with divine speech and action. Human and divine become at points inseparable. For many Jews, Christians, and Greco-Roman believers, the limits of human access to the supernatural were the limits of the human imagination.

Some of these rituals presumed a vast cosmos with dizzying layers of heavens full of entourages of angels—the higher and farther away from earth and matter, the better. In this multiheavened cosmology, a trip upward was a means for traversing the cosmos and gaining access to the upper regions where the deity dwelt. Escape was the goal, escape from all the bonds of earthly existence and life in the body, including fate, decay, and death.[1] The gap between heaven and earth was not just spatial. Heavenly existence was entirely different, and infinitely superior, to earthly existence.

1. This cosmology characterized by J. Z. Smith as "utopian" is described by Nilsson 1948:96–11. The contrasting "locative" view is described in the next paragraph.

For others, the world was far from the uppermost heavens, but it was still possible to find the highest spirit in the lowest level of existence. Nature held as much lure as the skies, but alignment, not escape, was the key.[2] Because the highest heavenly elements were available to humans in the lowest earthly elements, it was possible to work one's way upward from any point on the continuum. Ascent permitted the individual to join the upper realm, where he could participate in the heavenly world of the heavens along with its divine occupants.

This spectrum of beliefs produced a rich array of rituals, rituals that are evidence of the tremendous diversity of religious ideas at the turn of the millennium and in the centuries after. The rituals selected for this study stem primarily from Jewish texts, but they all have Christian and Greco-Roman parallels (first century B.C.E. to mid-fourth century C.E.). They were chosen both because they have been marginalized in modern scholarship and because they present a rich variety of ritual strategies, and they include ascents through the heavens, alchemical pursuits, and acts aimed at gaining special help with a variety of life issues, such as problems with love and personal advance. These are found in a variety of Hebrew and, secondarily, Greek texts, all of which are introduced chapter by chapter in the present volume.

The ritual texts, and the more speculative texts that develop the philosophical underpinning for rituals, do not present themselves as being magical, suspect, or in any way marginal vis-à-vis their religious traditions, but this does not mean that the rituals were without controversy. There are issues of secrecy and strict limitations of both knowledge and practice to select individuals and circles. The practitioners of these rites were no doubt enmeshed in debates about who was permitted to engage in them and who was not, and what the use of divine power implied. For example, in rabbinic circles we find evidence of hostile attacks about who was and was not permitted to make claims about what they had seen in the heavenly world.[3] Modern scholarship often presents the ancient debates about access to power as being a question of who engaged in "magic," but

2. This cosmology, characterized as "locative," represents a vision of the world that had been traditional since the time of the Ancient Near Eastern religions. See J. Z. Smith 1978: 1–13, 13–42, 147–51, 16–66, 169–71, 185–89, 291–94, 38–39.

this stance simply repeats the ancient prejudices without analyzing them and is thus rejected in this study.

While the thrust of this study is directed at elucidating the Jewish rituals, every chapter includes comparable rituals from other religious traditions (Christian and Greco-Roman). The reasons for this are many. First, the Jewish texts and the rituals they describe are often difficult, if not impossible, to date. For all these rituals, we depend on textual traditions that are fraught with problems. The Christian and Greco-Roman material is thus crucial in dating the Jewish ideas. Second, and in some ways more important, one theme of this study is that we can understand these rituals only when we look at them from a broader than usual base. These rituals reflect, so the argument goes, common ideas about efficacy. These ideas were shared across the boundaries of what we tend to think of as independent, and essentially distinct, religious traditions.

While these rituals may seem exotic to the reader, we shall see that they were based on the same notions of how rituals work as more familiar rites. The power of the divine name drives every Jewish blessing, and the Christian Eucharist is dependent on the transforming capability of words.

The ritual texts have been the source of much modern controversy, which in part reflects ancient debates about who is permitted to engage in these practices. The rituals were understood to be effective, but not necessarily permissible for everyone (as Chapter 1 explains). Ancient competitors—that is, other practitioners than those who preserved and copied the texts for us—sometimes labeled these rites "magic." To those who practiced them, all such actions were in the image of the deity.

This book seeks to rescue these rituals that modern scholarship, perpetuating some Late Antique biases, continues to denigrate, or mischaracterize, as "magic." The very term "magic," the source of so much recent controversy, is only one small piece of a complex map of ideas about how and why some rituals work and how and why others are less effective, less suitable, or wrong. Many modern scholarly studies of Late Antique rituals fall into the "Yes, but" category, first critiquing the term

3. See the discussion in Chapter 5.

"magic," then using it anyway.[4] This Introduction briefly reviews how the current categories used for classifying these texts ("magic" and "mysticism") have limited our engagement with them, and then introduces the methods used in this study.

It is beyond the scope of this book, and seems redundant to me, to rehearse the demise of classical twentieth-century definitions of "magic."[5] This study builds on the growing consensus that such labels as "magic" are inseparable from their pejorative use in the past. Modern writers cannot use the term as if it represented more than a polemical distinction about who was permitted to indulge in what activities.[6]

Nevertheless, some scholars of Late Antique Jewish rituals continue to use the label "magic," just as, for example, Ludwig Blau did in his 1914 *Das altjüdischen Zauberwesen*. Blau included as "magic" any references to the evil eye, powerful words, use of the divine name, amulets, mezuzahs, and exorcisms.[7] Other scholars have not missed the trenchant criticism of once-standard definitions of magic and are eager to embrace

---

4. H. S. Versnel accepts many of the critiques of traditional notions of magic but balks at totally abandoning substantive definitions (1991). He relies in the end on a "common sense" definition of magic, which includes the use of compulsive means in activities such as cursing. However, labeling a means "compulsive" is often subjective. Equally problematic is the idea of keeping certain types of unpleasant behavior such as cursing out of standard definitions of religion. C. R. Philips explicitly endorses a sociological definition of magic for the Late Antique world, but then explains that the lack of a more coherent definition was due to polytheism and its "receptive" nature (1986). A proper definition of religion and hence of magic, he argues, was only to be worked out after the Theodosian Code. Yet the internecine charges of magic between Protestants and Catholics belie a simple and consistent Christian definition of magic. Even Susan Garret in her laudable critique falls back on older definitions in such statements as "Although there were widespread prohibitions against it, magic flourished in the Greco-Roman world" (1989).

5. For an extremely lucid summary and critique, see Tambiah 1990.

6. For one recent analysis of how the term functions as a polemic, see Neusner 1989:61–81. See also Janowitz 2001:13–26.

7. This model is followed closely by Peter Schäfer, who includes as magic the use of seals, "magic" speech, amulets, and "magical" acts (1990). He does not explain what magical speech and acts are, but uses the terms liberally and makes it clear that they are by definition nonrabbinic. Describing one text discussed below (Chapter 5), he writes: "We are dealing with nothing less than a primitive hocus-pocus or abracadabra" (1992:165). Likewise, he writes about the heavenly journey and the adjuration of angels that "in both cases the means of achieving this is magic. The worldview that informs these texts is deeply magical. The authors of the hekhalot literature believed in the power of magic and attempted to integrate magic into Judaism" (1988a). For a similar usage, see Kern-Ulmer (1996).

new definitions. Hence, modifications have been made during the past decades to Blau's schema, primarily by reclassifying some of the items, such as the use of mezuzahs, as religion. The central theme left in the rapidly shrinking Blau model is the use of the divine name, which appears to be the last-gasp substantive definition of magic.[8] For this reason, attention is directed in this study toward the ideologies of the divine name, and an attempt is made to find a more precise way to describe its role.

In this study I also eschew the label "mysticism" for the texts, including the *hekhalot* (palace) texts analyzed in Chapter 5. A consistent definition of mysticism has never been formulated. In addition, the term sets up an implicit hierarchy of religious expression, much of which comes from Christian writers.[9] Mysticism means, for example, spiritual as opposed to legalistic modes of religious expression. The classical mystical worldview is usually connected with a specific cosmology, such as the Hellenistic one with its *deus abscondus* (absent god) in the seventh heaven or beyond. The search for communion or union with this far-off god becomes the core of mystical pursuit. Some religions, because they have other cosmologies with different structures for their interactions with divinity, end up being by definition "nonmystical" and thus lower forms of religious expression. For example, the religious expressions found in parts of the Hebrew Scriptures have suffered from this characterization, and even more so have "primitive" religions. Rather crudely put, the deity is too "close" to have extensive concern with the struggle for mystical communion. Communion with a far-off deity ends up being classified as a more spiritual experience than, for example, meeting a god at a tent or sitting down to a meal with a god.

8. For one example, among many, of magic consisting primarily of divine names, see Elior 1993:11. Schäfer distinguishes between an ascent to heaven based on ecstasy, and another that uses magical and theurgic means. This distinction rests entirely on calling the use of divine names "magic" (1992:154).

9. In his history of the term "mysticism," Boyer unwittingly shows the Christian bias in the shift from translating the Greek term *mystikos* not as "mysterious" but as "mystical" only when the term appears in the writings of church fathers. While the Jewish use is evaluated more highly than the pagan use, it still falls short and does not represent "mysticism" per se. Boyer explains that "with Philo it was merely a way of poeticizing about technical expositions of the most abstruse problems, with Clement and Origen it was generally employed for all that touched upon what was considered the most difficult theological problems presented by Christianity" (1980:45).

Yet another important theoretical problem with the term "mysticism" is the vast range of religious experiences which it conflates. Mysticism as a scholarly category grew in popularity in part because it appeared to offer an easy solution to the vexing problem of comparing religions. R. C. Zaehner found reassurance in his observation that "comparisons between mystical writings of quite divergent religions are at least comparisons between like and like" (1960:2). If orthodox theological doctrines look too particularistic for comparison, the experience of the sacred in its most generalized form is more easily compared. Everyone was presumed to experience the same ultimate reality.

These presumptions are now widely doubted. Steven Katz (1978, 1988) points out that there is no such thing as an unmediated religious experience. Stripping away the language in hopes of finding the pure experience it encodes cannot be done. To posit a phenomenological reality, "mysticism" presumes that the experiences "behind" the language used to describe it are of the same god, or, more ecumenically, the same Reality. However, as Hans Penner notes, "We must remember that all we have for understanding mysticism is language, not experience" (1983:91).

Huston Smith (1990) recounts a touching episode in which a visitor to America deposited money in a bank and then asked to have the very same dollar returned. Smith intimates that, unlike the misguided native, we correctly know that all dollars *really* are the same. This is a stunning demonstration of how positing a phenomenological "sameness" results in the loss of the meaning of a cultural artifact. Money does not function in every society as it does in America.[10]

Some have tried to shrink the theoretical claims entailed in the term "mysticism" by shifting the term from a noun to an adjective, emphasizing the "mystical" dimension of Judaism. Penner has critiqued this stance, arguing that the notion of a mystical aspect to a religious tradition still distorts the evidence (1983). Penner's particular example comes from Hinduism. The isolation of ascetic practices as the core of Hindu mysticism distorts the traditions because it separates asceticism from issues of caste. Asceticism and caste are two sides of the same coin. Placing Hindu

---

10. For an illuminating exchange between Katz and Smith, see Katz 1988.

ascetic practices next to ascetic practices from Christianity, for example, ignores the fact that choosing to be an ascetic is a choice to step out of the caste system. Without this context, we cannot understand what choosing to become an ascetic meant within the religious system. He concludes: "The mystical illusion is the result of an abstraction that distorts the semantic or structural field of a religious system. As such it is a false category, unreal, regardless of whether it is taken as the universal essence of religion or as a particular feature of a religious system" (1983:96).

From yet another point of view, Proudfoot points out that the term "mysticism" carries with it modes of evaluation. The term, therefore, comes with built-in explanations, as does, for example, the word "miracle." Thus the term cannot be used and explained in "naturalistic terms" (1985:137). Similarly, mystical experience is, "a phrase that includes among the rules for its proper application an explanatory commitment—namely, the judgment that whatever physiological or mental states are being identified as mystical could not be accounted for in naturalistic terms" (1985:139).

At the same time, the mystical experience is considered "authoritative, revelatory, and . . . support for the teachings of the tradition within which it is identified and interpreted" (1985:153). Scholars then have the odd task of choosing which religious experiences will be sanctioned as "mystical" and which other, nonmystical, experiences must be explained without recourse to any notion that they are grounded in some reality.

Finally, classifying a text as "mysticism" puts an emphasis on the experiential dimension of the texts. This is the most inherently elusive aspect of the material. because we have so little information about the experiences of those who used the texts. Despite this lack of information, questions of experience have dominated much recent debate.

The need for "mystical" Judaism derives from a once-dominant picture of Late Antique Judaism as legalistic, insular, and abstracted from the general historical context. Such scholars as Gershom Scholem argued the notion of Jewish mysticism in order to make room for modes of Jewish religious expression neglected by the previous generations of scholars. Ironically, this strategy now functions to keep the texts Scholem championed at the periphery of Jewish expression.

MODERN THEORIES OF RITUAL EFFICACY

The issue of the perceived efficacy of Late Antique rituals has two dimensions, and these supply the twin goals of the study as well as the grounds for discussion. The first goal is to illuminate how ancient practitioners understood their rituals to work. The second goal is to demonstrate that the semiotic vocabulary developed by modern anthropologists and philosophers of language offers us precise tools for analyzing the Late Antique ritual texts. These twin goals will necessitate shifting between some dense Late Antique texts and some equally dense modern terminology; each will be explained as carefully as possible.

The first goal implies many questions. Did the practitioners have theories to explain how and why their rituals worked? How were the various components of the ritual (the words said, the actions taken) understood to bring about the transformation of a person or a metal? Uncovering Late Antique ideas about rituals is not difficult; the challenge is to analyze these notions instead of simply adopting them. Ancient texts themselves sometimes express directly the ideologies that informed these rituals, as we shall see in the case of the Jewish exegetical texts discussed in Chapter 2.

One claim of this study is that we need better terminology for analyzing rituals than the Late Antique terms we have tended to recycle, which have been laden with Late Antique implications and modern polemics.[11] This drive for more precise terminology leads us perforce to the work of linguists and anthropologists as a source of unbiased tools for analysis. From the vast recent scholarship on ritual, this study draws on the work of S. J. Tambiah, Michael Silverstein, and Richard Parmentier, anthropologists who have developed the semiotic analysis of ritual.[12] Semiotics refers to the use of signs, a sign being something that stands for something else. Rituals are highly structured uses of signs that have complex relationships with their contexts of use. That is, they can "do things" to the world around them based on socially conceived models of efficacy. To pour oil on someone, to put on a special robe, to recite a formula, to point

11. For example, to state that pagans or polytheists engaged in magic, as so much modern scholarship does, is simply to repeat a Christian and/or Jewish polemical stance.

12. For introductions to these scholars, see in particular Tambiah 1985:17–59, 60–86, 123–66; Silverstein 1978 and 1993; and Parmentier 1994:128–34.

a scepter at someone—all these actions change the contexts in which they occur. In his article "A Performative Approach to Ritual," S. J. Tambiah in calls attention to the formality, stereotypy, condensation, and redundancy of ritual (1979:119). These aspects of ritual are often considered potentially negative, in contrast to, for example, spontaneous or unique events. Indeed, rituals are, to use Rappaport's wording, "among the most perfectly recurrent social events" (1992:14). Rituals can seem so rigid and devoid of meaning that they are simply declared meaningless. Oddly enough, the very aspects of ritual that appear so backwards turn out to offer a key to how rituals work. Formality does not always imply lack of coherence; the repetitive structure of poetry is a key to its ability to create new meanings. The ability of signs to affect the contexts in which they are used is dependent on the structures in which they are employed.

Tambiah argues, for example, that the repetitive patterning of rituals, which he calls "ritual involution," is a key to their function (1985: 123–66). The repetitious structures of a rite construct a model that is a copy of every prior rite leading back to the original model.[13] Each individual Eucharist reminds us, for example, of the original event on which it is patterned. It must resemble the original event closely enough for it to derive implications from that original event. As Parmentier explains, ritual actions "are not just conventional, they are so conventionalized that they highlight or call attention to the rules, that is, to the pattern, model, or semiotic type that the ritual actions instantiates (is an instance of)" (1994:133).

In religious rituals the original model includes the actions and words of a god or some type of supernatural figure. Each rite is one instance of a general type of socially conceived ritual action in which divine power is active. To the extent that rituals are based on culturally specific patterns, such putting into play of divine powers may be mystifying to outsiders, as well as insiders.

The repetitious structures of rituals not only point toward past events but also help create the settings for the rite. The language, and other signs, used in the rites construct the context for the successful completion of the

13. Thus even a "happening" must recreate the specific form of chaos based on the original "happening."

rite. The formal structure of ritual is in part an articulation of the "culturally-derived aspects of the cosmologies" (Tambiah 1985:142)—that is, the words spoken, and the objects used in rituals, construct for the participants the context they need for the rite to be successfully completed. We need to find ways of describing the context-creating ability of words and of objects, or, in the terms of this study, of all the various types of signs (semiotics) employed in rites.

On the issue of language, to the outsider ritual language often looks absurd because it appears to violate rules of semantics. It is highly repetitious or even nonsensical. Modern scholars of religion have tended to look askance, for example, at Late Antique ideas about divine names that diverge from our own "words are names for objects" (referential) model of language.[14] Late Antique ideas about the divine name, and other odd-sounding ideas about language we will encounter, are not oddities that defy any mode of analysis. Everyone who uses language is aware that, at times, words seem to "do things." The most well-known and influential formulation of this concept is J. L. Austin's *How to Do Things with Words* (1962). Among his most famous examples is the formula "I now pronounce you man and wife," which effects the marriage. Austin's study has been used by numerous scholars of ritual, including Tambiah. Austin distinguishes between several types of verbal acts, including illocutionary and perlocutionary acts; the latter are acts where the act is achieved by the utterance itself. His notion of "felicities" raises the question of the relationship between various formulas and the context of use and attempts to make systematic observations about these relationships.

This study does not use the particular terminology of Austin, but instead locates his ideas within a more general theory of the multifunctionality of language.[15] This theory about the different possible functions of language supplements the more familiar function of words as referential (semantics, how words refer to objects) with the less familiar notion of pragmatic functions. Pragmatic functions relate language to the contexts of use, much as Austin was attempting to do, but without his emphasis on certain verbal forms. Thus, pragmatic speech refers to speech that affects

14. See Silverstein 1976 for a discussion of the referential drive in linguistic theory.
15. For Austin's limitations, see Silverstein 1978.

the context in which it is spoken—that is, speech that has consequences in the real world. These linguistic functions lead us to the heart of ritual, because ritual formulas (and other linguistic units) influence the context in which they are spoken.[16]

These functions of language are not unique to ritual. S. J. Tambiah named his article the punning "Magical Power of Words" in order to point out that this property belongs to words in general. One place to begin thinking about the functions of language is with legal language. In certain social contexts, for example, words are understood to effect contracts. These functions of language are culturally specific. They necessitate in turn a meta-system—that is, a set of rules that clarify and delineate how and when words work (function in this way). Much of the training in law school has to do with getting students to move beyond the "semantic-interpretive orientation" they learned in previous schooling (Mertz 1996). The students practice for example, oral exchange and debate, thereby learning the rules for the special language uses associated with law. The students need to grasp such notions as precedent and procedural history. All these are meta-level concepts that determine what can be done with the words of law. As Elizabeth Mertz explains, "A legal reading of case law focuses on the metapragmatics of the text, in which lies the key to its authority" (1996:236).

So too the function of political oratory is often not simply what the political speech is "about." As one example among many, Parmentier analyzes for us the political speech that a high-ranking titleholder in Belauan society gave during a crisis in the village. In this speech the titleholder sought to bring about a resolution to the crisis not so much by talking about the resolution as by enacting it in his very performance (1994:96).

Repeatedly in law, politics, and religious rituals, we are reminded that semantics is not the be-all-and-end-all of language. The general notion that words "stand for" objects—which is the basis of semantics—will not suffice. The patterns, or models, of rituals are replete with intricate and bewildering uses of words and other signs that are less familiar modes of representation. We must have ways of describing the rules by which

16. For a detailed discussion of the many distinct functions of language, see Silverstein 1993.

words and objects "stand for" other things in these rituals: how an image "stands for" the person against whom a rite is directed, how a name "stands for" a divine presence, how incense "stands for" a cosmic exchange. If we are going to do anything other than guess at the meaning of these rituals we need a way to articulate exactly how these "standings for" work and how they differ among themselves.

This study uses the sign system developed by C. S. Peirce to delineate modes of representation (1940).[17] For those dissatisfied with the vague concepts of "symbol" found so often in the analysis of religion, Peirce offers a detailed analysis of how signs stand for objects.[18]

A sign does not simply "stand for" an object in the familiar way in which, for example, a name stands for an object. Instead, for a sign to have meaning it must include a triadic relationship between the object itself, a sign that represents that object, and an interpretant—that is, the "translation, explanation, meaning or conceptualization of the sign-object relation in a subsequent sign representing the same object" (Parmentier 1994:5). Each sign "stands for" its object in different ways, depending on the particular relationship between the three dimensions of the sign (object, sign, and interpretant). The specific terms Peirce uses for the three distinct ways of "standing for" are "icon," "index," and "symbol."[19] Peirce defines the first type of sign, "icon," as "a sign which would possess the character which renders it significant, even though the object had no existence; such as a lead pencil streak in representing a geometrical line" (1940:14). If we think about the example of the line, its form is important, indeed crucial, to its function. Alter the form, and the meaning is altered.

Icons are not arbitrary in the way that we generally think of words as collections of sounds arbitrarily chosen to represent an object. All icons

17. Peirce's succinct essay "Logic as Semiotic: The Theory of Signs" is a good summary of his theory (1940:98–119). For a clear introduction to Peirce, see Parmentier 1994:3–44. See also Sheriff 1989 for a short introduction and some examples of application.

18. See, for example, Asad's critique (1993:3) of Geertz's concept of symbol as being inadequately defined in Geertz's influential definition of religion. Asad contrasts Geertz's vagueness with the precision of Peircean terminology.

19. The term "symbol" is thus preserved for a specific kind of signifying relationship. Here Peirce believed he was returning to a definition of "symbol" that was closer to its ancient usage based on the Greek root "to throw together."

have formal resemblances to the entities they represent. Maps are iconic; if they were totally arbitrary they would not be much help in finding one's way. International signs try to be as iconic as possible so that people from a variety of cultures can understand them. Hence the iconic representations of men and women on bathroom doors.

In the world of law, one example of an icon is a personal signature. In the American legal system it is necessary to establish one's signature. The standard way this is done is by signing what is known as a signature guarantee—a paper that states that a certain signature is in fact one's signature. Once that icon, the signature, is established it is a legally binding representation of that person.

Deities are also represented in rituals by means of culturally specific notions of, as it were, signature guarantees. These icon signs are especially important because they establish divine presences in rituals. Any ritual in which a deity is believed to be present will have some form of iconic representation of that deity—that is, the deity is not simply referred to in a ritual, but is physically present in some sign with formal links to the deity.

Peirce's second type of sign is an index that is linked to what it stands for by a "pointing" relationship, such as smoke to fire, or a weather vane to wind. For this type of representation, a sign must be in spatial-temporal contiguity with that which it represents. Someone yelling "Come here!" can be understood only when "here" is made clear by the context.

Establishing "pointing to" relationships is important in rituals, because it links all the components that are part of the ritual setting—including, for example, human participants and divinities. The "here" in which a particular ritual takes place is established by the very ritual itself, where the setting is created, whether it is a room in which a deity is believed to live or one of the highest heavens.

The symbol, the third type of sign, has an arbitrary relationship with that which it represents, and lacks both the formal and spatial relations of the other signs. American stop signs are arbitrarily chosen to represent the concept of stopping at a cross street. Given this arbitrary relationship, the form of the symbol is not motivated by its sign in any way. These signs are based entirely on social convention and thus vary from culture to culture.

Words, for example, are based on social convention.[20] Symbols are likely to have complex and shifting clusters of meaning that are difficult to understand in cross-cultural contexts.[21]

While this terminology may seem cumbersome at first, many of the rituals discussed below are predicated on the distinct semiotic function of certain signs. It is impossible to understand this function of the divine name, and to compare it with other possible ways in which words and signs can function, without the very specific semiotic vocabulary of icon, index, and symbol. The larger iconic structures of ritual texts also turn out to be crucial.

Abstracted from their contexts, many of these uses of signs will look like nonsensical, misdirected actions (hocus-pocus), just as legal texts sound like gobbledy-gook to the uninitiated. Consider how much more so this will be the case for religious rituals, where many of the forces involved in the rituals are themselves represented by signs because of their very nature (invisible gods and so on). Without these icons and indices, rituals would be empty, because the divine powers are accessible to humans to the extent that their signs are manifest or point to their presence. Anytime a deity acts it will be via the semiotic signs (wine, name, angel) that "stand for" the deity.

This book uses these tools to investigate how rituals were considered effective modes of social action in the Late Antique period, however they may appear to us now. What captured the imagination of Late Antique practitioners was the perceived efficacy of the rituals. Much of the contemporary debate about these rituals (real versus literary, magical versus mystical versus religious) falls by the wayside when we are able to articulate the perceived efficacy of the rituals in their historical contexts.

This study describes both how ancient practitioners believed rituals worked and how modern semiotic theory can illuminate the rituals. Sometimes the connections between the worlds of theory and of practice in the Late Antique evidence are tenuous or difficult to discern, and often we

20. An interesting exception is onomatopoetic words, which are believed to be formally linked to what they represent.

21. When a meaning is easily located, it may be because the symbol is in effect "dead." See Parmentier 1994:47–69.

lack clear theoretical texts (there are more extant Christian and Greco-Roman theoretical texts than Jewish). Even in these cases it is still possible to connect rituals to the historical context and its ideas of efficacy, and thereby avoid relying on the sweeping generalizations that have dominated contemporary discussions of magic and ritual. How was it that rituals are able to reach the lofty goals outlined at the beginning of this Introduction? Only an analysis of the pragmatics of Late Antique rituals will help us answer this question.

ABBREVIATIONS

Ber   Marcellin Berthelot and C. Ruelle, *Collection des anciens alchimiste grecs.* 1888. Reprint, London: Holland Press, 1963.

PG   J. P. Migne, *Patrologia graeca.* Parisiis: Migne, 1857–66.

PGM   K. Preisendanz, ed., *Papyri graecae magicae* (Greek Magical Papyri). Stuttgart: Teubner, 1928–31.

PL   J. P. Migne, *Patrologia latina.* Parisiis: Migne, 1844–91.

I

LATE ANTIQUE THEORIES
OF EFFICACY

Rituals work by faith, truth, and love
—Proclus *Commentary on Alcibiades* 357.12

Paradoxically, rituals that claim to reveal divinity on earth can look to outsiders as if their purpose is to manipulate that same divine power. The difference is in the eye of the beholder. Similarly, distinguishing between the work of an angel and a daimon, between the work of good forces and evil forces is a subtle, if not impossible, task. (I am using the word "daimon" and not "demon" to emphasize that in Late Antiquity these beings were not always evil.) Even if everyone agrees, for example, that someone was healed, that does not preclude variant explanations of exactly what happened. Hostile outsiders and internal opponents are apt to levy charges against practices and rituals that look suspicious to them, even if they admit that the rituals work.

In late antiquity, the word "magic" (Greek μαγεία, Latin *magia*) was widely used in intergroup and intragroup polemics. For the Persians, their word for "priest," *magos,* did not have any of the negative connotations it accrued in Greek culture. Beginning in the sixth century B.C.E., however, the term was associated in Greek literature with beggars and wizards.[1] this usage became standard despite a few references that more closely followed its historical origin, such as in Cicero.

It is not surprising that Christians denounced Jewish rituals as magic[2]

---

1. For the development of the Greek and Latin usages, see Graf 1997:2–6 and Janowitz 2001:9–13.

2. Jewish practices that were considered magic include fasting, dietary laws, and Sabbath observance. For Justin, all Jewish rituals are magic and identical to pagan rites, with their "magical fumigations and incantations" (*Dialogue with Trypho* 85.3). John Chrysostom's denunciations claimed, among other things, that daimons live in synagogues (*Homilies Against the Judaizers* 1.6). The Council of Laodicaea prohibited "Judaizing," which was understood as the adoption of magical practices, including the use of phylacteries (Canon 35–37).

while Jews denounced Jesus as a magician.[3] Representatives of both groups considered pagan rituals to be magic, and this equation helped determine that many of the rituals currently labeled "magic" are simply pagan rituals.[4] No doubt pagans believed that both Christianity and Judaism were permeated with magic, as the small amount of extant evidence demonstrates.[5] Opponents within a community were often tarred with the label "magician" in attempts to marginalize them, much as the term "heretic" was used.[6]

The stakes in these debates were high; magic was associated with dangerous and barbaric practices, real and imagined, including human sacrifice and cannibalism.[7] Pliny the Elder matter-of-factly stated that magical rites involve killing and eating men (*Natural History* 30.13). In addition to the negative associations, the practice of magic was a criminal offense under Roman law (Iulius Paulus *Excerpts* 5.23.14–18). To be accused of practicing magic had all the drama of modern charges of high treason and could have lethal results.

Much of this charge and countercharge can be correctly characterized

---

3. Many of the Jewish texts were censored, and thus it is difficult to reconstruct references to Jesus. See the discussion in M. Smith 1978:46–55.

4. For the standard equation of paganism with magic and suspect practices of all types found in the writings of the Christian apologists, see Thee 1984:328. For Justin, for example, becoming a Christian was a turn away from magic (*First Apology* 14.2). See Pseudo-Clementine *Homilies* 5.4–7; Clement *Exhortation* 1 and *The Teacher* 3.4. Simon 1986:361–62.

5. For Christian rituals that looked magical to pagans, see, for example, Suetonius *Nero* 16.2 and the comments of Celsus preserved by Origen in *Against Celsus*. For the common pagan equation of Judaism and magic, see, for example, Juvenal's denunciation of Jewish oracles (*Satire* 6.546), Lucian of Samosata's reference to Jewish incantations (*The Gout Tragedy*, 171–73), Celsus' statement that Jews are addicted to magic (*Against Celsus* 1.26), Posidonius' claim that Jews were sorcerers (Strabo *Geography* 16.2.43), and Pliny's statement that magic comes from the Jews (*Natural History* 30.11). In a modern continuation of this stereotype in what is otherwise a very sophisticated discussion, Simon appears to accept the idea that in the Late Antique world Jews were magicians and infected early Christianity with magic. He writes, "Though it is true that Judaism, by means of its theodicy and its morality, was able to seduce the noblest of the pagans, it also exercised a more murky influence on the masses by its reputed ability to ward off the Powers" (1986:341).

6. See the accusations of magic made against Christian rivals, such as Marcus, Simon, and Menander, in the writings of Irenaeus (see *Against the Heresies* 1.13.1).

7. The connection between "magoi" and human sacrifices goes back to Herodotus *Histories* 7.114.

as "your ritual is magic, mine is religion" (Neusner 1989). But that does not exhaust Late Antique period debates about magic. A full discussion of the use of the term "magic" in late antiquity is beyond the scope of this chapter.[8] The most important point that needs to be made here has to do with efficacy: magic was believed to be effective. No doubt there were some individuals who rejected any supernatural interventions in daily life, but such people were rare. For most Late Antique writers the term usually implied potentially effective but nonetheless inappropriate uses of divine powers. Either the wrong powers were put to work (evil demons) or the wrong people were engaged in using the powers (outsiders, women, and the like).

The other half of this highly polemical debate, which will occupy this chapter, was the attempt by some Greco-Roman thinkers both to defend specific rituals and explain the use of rituals in general. While these issues were of great importance to diverse Late Antique thinkers, the discussions among the Neoplatonists are particularly lucid and well developed. These thinkers wrote commentaries on Plato's dialogues and other writings during the second through fifth centuries C.E. The explanation of ritual that interests us specifically is the development of theories of "theurgy," a term that is parallel to theology (words about divinity) but that has the emphasis on effective action.

E. R. Dodds developed the standard conception, still widely cited, for the meaning of the term "theurgy" (1947). Dodds used two closely connected approaches to define it, first defining it as religious ends reached through magical means and then delineating it as a specific set of rituals (animation of statues, divination by means of mediums). In the last few decades the inadequacy of Dodds' schema of theurgy, which was based on a rigid evolutionary model of religion and magic, has been repeatedly emphasized. Dodds did not invent this evolutionary schema; his contribution was to characterize Plotinus as a philosopher representing the top of the hierarchy, and theurgy, sharing methods with magic, as the lowest form of religion. Dodds had a decidedly antiritual stance in general, setting Plotinus sharply against an irrational environment enmeshed in ridiculous rit-

8. See Janowitz 2001:9–26.

uals.[9] Dodds's definition has unraveled as scholars realized that the list was too short and began adding additional elements. Georg Luck's reconstruction of the theurgic ritual now includes periods of silence, references to a "warming fire," manipulation of material objects and writing down of things, use of tools, and drugs or mind-altering substances (Luck 1989:192–93).[10] It is to Luck's credit that he has moved theurgy from the fringe of pagan practice to its center, thereby making imperative a reconsideration of its relationship to traditional paganism. But his definition is so broad that it delineates no clear set of rituals.

As the review below demonstrates, the rituals associated with theurgy by ancient writers were for the most part quite old.[11] That is, the term referred not so much to a new set of "magical" techniques but rather to a hodgepodge of some older rituals (for instance, animating statues, prayer, and animal sacrifice) and some newer rituals (for instance, ascents through the heavens). What was new was that these rites were granted the philosophical imprimatur of "theurgy." Our argument is the opposite of Luck's recent statement, "The need of pagan believers to enter into direct contact with their gods led to the development of a certain technique or a set of techniques codified during the reign of Marcus Aurelius, it seems, and given the name "theurgy'" (1989:185). On the contrary, the main import of calling a rite "theurgy" is the new interpretations of ritual efficacy it articulated. These new interpretations explain how the specific techniques, and rituals in general, work.

The term "theurgy" was not only aimed at skeptical outsiders, nor is that necessarily its origin. In addition to deflecting charges of "magic," discussions of theurgy explain rituals in light of shifting attitudes toward specific rituals and the resulting need to constantly update them. Explaining theurgy leads us deep into issues of ritual efficacy and helps paint a background against which to consider the rituals discussed in the chapters below.

9. Gregory Shaw has the most insightful critique of the antiritual bias of much scholarly work (1985:9). Athanassiadi's recent discussion is corrective of Dodds but is only for Iamblichus. The issue of a general definition remains.

10. As the category "magic" shrinks, the category "theurgy" blossoms.

11. Dodds acknowledges this in his highly influential article, though he still presents theurgy as a new type of quasi-magical expression (1947:63).

LATE ANTIQUE CONCEPTS OF THEURGY

As reported by his friend Iamblichus (250–325 C.E.), the Neoplatonic thinker Porphyry (232–305 C.E.) raised questions about the philosophical basis of ritual. "How is it that rituals work?" Porphyry pondered. He had been trained by Plotinus, who believed that many components of traditional religion were not theoretically grounded. Porphyry was daring to ask why one would bother to pray, or do any other ritual.

In response, Iamblichus argued that it was impossible to proceed to the goal of unity with divinity without ritual actions.[12] He chided Porphyry for trying to solve every problem with dialectics (*On the Mysteries* 10.1–7; 285.10–293.13). Those who only talk and employ dialectics will never achieve the contact with divinity they all sought. "It is not thought that links the theurgist to gods; else what should hinder the theoretical philosopher from enjoying theurgic union with them? This case is not so. Theurgic union is attained only by the perfective operation of ineffable acts, correctly performed acts which are beyond all understanding, and by the power of the unutterable symbols which are intelligible only to the gods" (2.11; 96.13–97.2). It would be difficult to improve on this statement as a contemporary explanation of ritual efficacy. Rituals, Iamblichus explains, do not always make sense to humans, even to insiders, but they do make sense to the gods. The gods send down instructions to complete certain actions that look strange to humans but that "perfect" humans. These acts provide what the dialecticians lack in their investigation of divinity.

The comment of Iamblichus that some aspects of ritual may be incomprehensible on the surface reappears in early uses of the term "theurgy." In what may be the earliest extant use of the word, Nicomachus of Gerasa (fl. c. 50–150 C.E.), who wrote a number of technical treatises, including "Introduction to Arithmetic," "Introduction to Geometry," and a manual on harmony and was a seminal figure in philosophical circles, uses the term "theurgists" in an explanation of why seemingly nonsensical vowel

---

12. The most important recent work on Iamblichus and theurgy is Shaw 1995. In particular, Shaw demonstrates how Iamblichus' theory of the descent of the soul meshed with his ideas about theurgy.

sounds are uttered in rituals.[13] Vowels are imitations of planet sounds, he explains, and thus are effective in rituals. He sets up an analogy between soul : body and vowel : consonant, arguing that unpronounceable vowels must be "clothed" in consonants in order to be used.[14] Once given materiality, they can be employed as powerful forces in ritual.[15] Nicomachus is arguing that vowels are a special kind of sign. This is only one instance of complex Neoplatonic philosophical discussions that insist that certain aspects of language are existentially connected with cosmic reality.[16] In Nicomachus' terms the vowels function "symbolically." In the Peircian terms of this study, the vowels function iconically, because each sound is a formal equivalent to the sound of a planet. Uttering the sounds brings the power of that force directly into the ritual.

The specific practices of these "theurgists" are not elaborated here. Whatever these rituals entailed, Iamblichus claimed they were "perfective of divine things." Surely for Nicomachus, as for Iamblichus, these are the most important rituals, though they are also likely to be misunderstood.

Other early uses of the term "theurgy" are associated with a father-and-son team of Julians who lived during the reign of Marcus Aurelius (161–68 c.e.).[17] The elder Julian is called a philosopher in the Suda entry under his name (*Suda* 1.433, s.v. Julianus).[18] The younger is remembered as the author of esoteric tractates including Theurgika/Θεουργικα (1.434). Anecdotes about the father and son depict them as champions of flashy rituals. "They say about him that once, when the Romans were exhausted by thirst, he suddenly caused dark clouds to gather and discharge torrential rain with incessant thunder and lightning; and that Julian worked this by some wisdom" (1.433). These actions were apt to be considered magic in the eyes of their opponents. Our picture of their practices is dependent

13. Dodds 1961:271 n. 31 rejects the term as a later addition, but his argument is not convincing.

14. Nicomachus on sounds is also discussed below in Chapter 4.

15. For further discussion of sounds in rituals, see Chapter 5.

16. See Stephen Gersh 1978 and the comments in Chapter 4 on Neoplatonic theories about letters.

17. For recent reviews of the dating problems and the evidence about the father and son, see E. des Places (1984) and G. Fowden (1987). H. D. Saffrey (1981) is skeptical of much of the biographical data, contra H. Lewy (1978).

18. The Suda is a historical encyclopedia derived from more ancient scholarship, compiled at the end of the tenth century.

on these writers, many of whom had no great sympathy for the Julians. For these writers, "theurgy" is indistinguishable from "magic."

The rituals attributed to the father-son team were not new or unique to the Julians.[19] They were embraced by their followers not so much for their novelty as for their presumed success with manifesting divinity on earth. The elder Julian was said to be able to make Plato's soul speak through a human medium, "conjoining" his son "with the gods and with Plato's soul."[20] H. D. Saffrey, who rejects most of the biographical data, accepts the idea that the father used his son as a medium to receive oracles from Plato (1981:218–19). The father could bring about an appearance of the god Chronos (Proclus *Commentary on the Timaeus* 3.20.22), separate his body from his soul (Proclus *Commentary on the Republic* 2.123.9–1), and heal.[21] They were renowned for a rain miracle, which in some versions included use of a human mask that cast thunderbolts at the enemy.[22] Fowden's careful analysis of the thunderbolt episode demonstrates that the story may originally have been attributed to another famous pagan figure and only later attributed to Julian by his followers (Fowden 1987).

The text most closely associated with the Julians is the patchy collection of enigmatic verses known as the *Chaldean Oracles*.[23] This text, reconstructed first by Kroll and later by des Places, is still the source of much controversy. Johnston concludes, "Despite the murkiness that surrounds the Juliani, the *Oracles* emerged during the mid to late second century (1990:3).

The extant fragments from the *Chaldean Oracles* do not include the word "theurgy," but one fragment explains, "Theurgists do not fall into the herd which is subject to destiny" (frag. 153). Engaging in theurgy thus elevates one above the common people, and even cosmic forces. The fragments urge the reader to engage in various rituals. One fragment calls specifically for a combination of "action (ἔργον) with sacred word

19. See note 11.

20. Psellus *The Golden Chain*, ed. Sathas 1875:217; French translation in Leveque 1959:79. Julian also was said to have prayed that his son have the soul of an archangel.

21. In a medieval Christian legend, Julian competes with two other healers, Apollonius and Apuleius, to end a plague in Rome (Anastasius of Sinai *Quaestiones* [PG 89, col. 252ab]).

22. The mask version is preserved in Psellus *Minor Writings* 1.446.8–447.14 K-D; see des Places 1971:221–22.

23. See Lewy 1978 and the additions by des Places 1983. For a recent critical study, see Majercik 1989.

(λογος)" (110).[24] An inventory of the specific techniques mentioned in the *Oracles* nets a rich list. We find mention of an invocation or calling on the gods (7), which may or may not be related to the standard technique of reciting divine names (150).[25] The writings also describe the consecration of a statue of Hecate (224), use of a ritual wheel called a στρόφαλος (206, 208),[26] breathing techniques (123, 124), periods of silence (132), and sprinkling of water (133). Fragment 135 mentions a process of initiation. The status of animal sacrifice in the *Oracles* is debated; the only "sacrifice" directly discussed is that of a stone (149).[27] In a suspect fragment, Hecate appears in response to prayer (222).[28]

It seems unlikely that these references to ritual actions were all part of one specific "theurgic" ritual;[29] instead, they were probably part of distinct rituals, many of which, again, were traditional Greco-Roman religious practices. The officiant is referred to as "ἰερεὺς/priest" (frag. 133) and the participant as "μύστης/initiate" (132), both traditional terms.[30] The traditional practices likely were supplemented by some new rituals that reflected Late Antique cosmological concerns, primarily rituals of ascent (ἄνοδος) of the soul to the heavenly realm.[31]

The author of the *Oracles* distinguished his favorite rituals from other rituals he had rejected. The latter rituals included the use of birds and en-

24. For a discussion of shifting combination of words and actions in rituals, see the Concluding Note.

25. Several other fragments appear to be about divine names, including fragment 87, which describes a holy name leaping into the world, and fragments 76 and 77.

26. Majercik translates the term as "magical wheel," but the word "magic" does not occur in the text.

27. This appears to be some form of reinterpreted sacrifice. Lewy (1978:289) cites Psellus' statement that the "Chaldeans" offered up animals (*Minor Writings* 1.446.23). See also Lewy's Excursus 8 (1978:487–89).

28. For epiphanies of Hecate, see Johnston 1990:111–33.

29. Lewy reconstructed them as one ritual he considered a form of magic, as noted in the title of his chapter "The Magical Ritual of the Chaldeans" (1978:227–57). The nine elements of the ritual he outlined include, among others, "conjunction" with the gods, supplication, conjuring Hecate, consecrating a statue to Hecate, using a noise-making top, and divination.

30. Johnston outlines parallels between the language of the Oracles and terms from the mystery religions, though no doubt these terms appeared in a number of religious settings (1997:176–77).

31. Argued by Lewy 1978 and subsequently by Johnston 1997. She places an ascent ritual at both the core of the *Oracles* and thus her notion of "theurgy." For a broader discussion of ascent, see Chapter 5.

trails for divination (frag. 107), which are called "supports of a deceptive trade (ἐμποριψῆς ἀπάτης στηρίγματα)." The brief reference to "deceptive" ritual is a tantalizing hint about modes of categorizing rituals. "Deceptive" may mean that the rituals appear to work but are at some level fraudulent.

The *Oracles* represent not so much a new set of techniques as a grounding for a set of older techniques. Though abstruse, they present a theological system for the rituals that is replete with Platonic imagery (see Johnston 1997:169). Just as theology designates the very highest level of discourse about the gods, in the *Oracles* "theurgists" engage in a group of highly valued, traditional rituals with divine backing.

The first explicit definition of theurgy occurs in the writings of Porphyry, whom we encountered briefly above worrying about the theoretical basis of ritual. Porphyry could not settle on a philosophy that sufficiently explained the workings of rituals. This was true even for rituals aimed at achieving their most cherished goal of divine contact. In an excerpt preserved in Augustine, Porphyry states that by means of certain "theurgic consecrations (*teletai*), the spiritual element of the soul is put into a proper condition, capable of welcoming spirits and angels, and of seeing the gods" (Augustine *City of God* 10.9). "Consecration" or "initiation" (τελεω) was a traditional term for religious rituals.[32] The importance of theurgic consecrations is that they can attain a very lofty goal, which in Porphyry's case was to condition the soul to see the gods.

Porphyry's concept of ritual efficacy is carefully articulated and restricted. As with the *Oracles,* not all rituals are viewed as equal. Augustine preserves some of Porphyry's cautions and hesitations: "In fact he [Porphyry] says that the rational soul (or, as he prefers, the intellectual soul) can escape into its own sphere, even without any purification of the spiritual element by means of 'theurgic art,' and further, that the purification of the spiritual part by theurgy does not go so far as to assure its attainment of immortality and eternity" (*City of God* 10.9).

Ritual activity is not necessary for Porphyry's highest goals, nor is the success of even the best rituals ensured. Porphyry's theory does not mean

---

32. The term is connected, for example, with the mysteries of Demeter (Herodotus *Histories* 2.171).

that theurgic consecration can reach only modified goals while some *other* type of ritual can reach higher ones. It is a statement about the limitations of ritual in general. And theurgic acts of purification are not unique in their ability to help the soul. Unfortunately, however, we cannot tell from Porphyry's brief statement preserved in Augustine what else helps the soul escape to its sphere.

The highest goal, liberation of the soul, could be sought by means of rituals *to the extent that* there is a theoretical explanation of the efficacy of these rituals. The very best rituals, theurgy, can be of some help to individuals, but at the same time rituals with no conceptual basis are mere magic.[33] The potential of even "theurgy" was open to doubt. Until the efficacy of rituals is explained, all rituals look like magic. And for Porphyry it is folly to try to put magical constraints on the gods (Eusebius *Preparation for the Gospels* 5.10.199).

Iamblichus, who tried to answer Porphyry's doubts, did not necessarily plan to develop a philosophical defense of ritual, but he ended up developing one anyway.[34] Iamblichus' real concern, he tried to explain to his dialogue partner, was to illuminate the relationship of the human soul to the cosmos. Porphyry believed that the soul shunned any actions that look to the world and try instead to remain always in the upper cosmic realm. The soul could save itself without having to "do" anything, without having to engage in any type of ritual action. In Iamblichus' eyes, this was a frontal attack on traditional Platonic thought and threatened to lead people away from the gods.

For Iamblichus, moving toward the gods was the purpose of traditional practices, including even animal sacrifice (*On the Mysteries* 5.11; 215.3–7). He is particularly clear that these rituals do not work by compelling the gods.[35] The person performing the rituals must have the correct "inner disposition,"[36] a necessary condition, but not a sufficient one, for it does not legitimate or guarantee every type of ritual. He separated effec-

---

33. Johnston writes that Porphyry "also apparently recognized a level of theurgy concerned not at all with spiritual salvation but with more worldly, immediate goals" (1990:79). Perhaps it is more clear to state that according to Porphyry rituals can be directed toward a variety of goals, including some that may look surprisingly mundane to us.

34. As has been so elegantly argued by Gregory Shaw (1995).

35. See *On the Mysteries* 2.11; 96.13—97.9.

36. See A. Smith's discussion (1974:99), commented on by Shaw (1985:25).

tive ritual (theurgy) from false ritual (magic) based on an inner attitude toward the gods or spiritual disposition. Iamblichus' defense of this position foreshadows a mode of classifying true versus false ritual still used in religious polemics today.

Iamblichus revealed his philosophical snobbery in his rejection of "sympathy." According to this Late Antique cliché, divine processes exist on earth in hidden forms despite the apparent gulf between the deity and the material world. Earthly "symbols" can be manipulated so that they reveal divinity. Sympathy does exist, he admits, but it does not explain everything (*On the Mysteries* 5.7–9; 207.7–210.14). According to Iamblichus, divination by sympathy is "entirely different" from real theurgy (6.4; 244.13–245.10).[37]

Rituals Iamblichus rejects are labeled, as expected, "magic," for these cannot by definition have any spiritual or pious aspect (*On the Mysteries* 3.26; 161.10–16). In particular, he denounced the animation of statues as fraudulent and called makers of images "magicians" (3.25; 160.15).[38] The study of animal entrails and observation of the stars are mere human sciences (3.15; 135–136.10), while theurgy is not.

Proclus (b. 410/12) continued Iamblichus' positive evaluation of some rituals and attempted to explain the theoretical value of the rituals. His definition of "theurgy" is noteworthy in its total lack of reference to specific rituals. Theurgy is "a power higher than all human wisdom embracing the blessings of divination, the purifying powers of initiation and in a word all the operations of divine possession" (*Platonic Theology* 1.26.63).[39] Human wisdom cannot reach as high as divine power. Humans who enact rituals copy the gods, because gods "illuminate by actions and not by words" (4.26.220).

Proclus' promotion of ritual, expressed here, is supplemented and ex-

---

37. See Shaw 1985:204–5 and 233.

38. Dodds points out a secondhand report that Iamblichus believed statues contained divine presences (1947:64). Porphyry wrote a treatise titled *About Statues* that included symbolic interpretations of the statues of deities, the objects they hold, their stances, and so on (Bidez 1964: appendix 1). It is difficult to discern from the fragments whether he claimed that divine powers are present in the statues. Eunapius recounts how Maximus made a statue of a goddess smile, and the varied views of this type of activity (*Lives of the Philosophers* 475). Animation of statues is also associated with the Chaldeans by Psellus *Letter* 187 (see Lewy 1978:496).

39. See also *Platonic Theology* 1.25.113.

panded on in his various treatises. His treatise *Elements of Theology*, which supplies, in the words of Dodds, "the philosophical basis for theurgy" (1963:276)[40] is an abstract text and does not refer to specific rituals at all.[41] That is, the propositions explain the theoretical principles on which all successful rituals rest and do not support any particular ritual. Proposition 145, for example, states: "The distinctive character of any divine order travels through all the derivative existents and bestows itself upon all the inferior kinds" (1963:129). Even the most "inferior" level of existence has a distinctive character that connects it with the highest level, meaning that it is possible to work with the inferior level and affect the higher levels.

Rituals attributed to Proclus by his biographer, many of them familiar by now, include weather manipulation, evocation of a vision of Hecate, and participation in a ritual of divine communion called "σύστασις" (conjunction).[42] Statues can give revelations; gods make them speak the future (*On the Timaeus* 3.155.18–25).[43] A meeting of soul and divinity takes place in prayer, which no doubt explains Proclus' own practice of praying three times a day (Marinus *Life of Proclus* 22). And the liturgy probably included recitation of divine names, because "it is these names which theurgy expresses in imitating them by exclamations, sometimes distinct, sometimes indistinct" (*Commentary on the Cratylus* 71, p. 31).[44] Theurgists are taught the names of gods by the divine powers.[45] Ascent was also among Proclus' ritual practices; at the age of forty-two, he proclaimed that his soul had arrived in the heavens, which resound with immortality (Marinus *Life of Proclus* 28). Rituals he rejected are labeled "magic."[46] It is clear that for Proclus theurgic rituals are not com-

---

40. Shaw (1985:11) points to the importance of proposition 57 for understanding the philosophical basis for ritual.

41. As Dodds noted (1963:xvii).

42. Marinus *Life of Proclus* 28 (*Oracles,* frag. 28). See H. Lewy 1978:228–38.

43. See note 38 above.

44. Explaining this quotation, Dillon writes: "Theurgy teaches us how to represent the structure of the symbola in the physical world by means of inarticulate utterances" (1985:29). All nonsense is not theurgy, however, and not all theurgy uses nonsense.

45. *Commentary on the Timaeus* 1.274.16; see also *On the Cratylus* 72.8 and *Platonic Theology* 1.29.124.

46. *Commentary on the Republic* 1.255.19 and 1.29.14.

pulsive or manipulative magic, but represent the best of traditional ritual practices.[47]

Some Christians adopted similar usage and employed the term "theurgy" to refer to divine action or the most effective and powerful rituals. In an early liturgy, God is said to display "theurgic power (τῇ θεουργικῇ σου δυνάμει)" in miracles.[48] Theurgic power is the opposite of "magic" because it is divine. Dionysius the Areopagite, a fifth-century Christian writer we will meet again, was particularly enamored of the term; "theurgy" appears forty-seven times in his corpus and follows the Neoplatonic usage very closely.[49] The most significant ritual for him was, of course, the Eucharist, and this he calls theurgy. "Theurgics," he explained, are the consummation of theology (*Ecclesiastical Hierarchy* 3.5.432B), which is necessary because it is impossible to rise up toward the deity without material symbols (*Celestial Hierarchy* 1.3.121CD).

For other Christians, attacking "theurgy" was a way of attacking the heart of "pagan" beliefs and practice. For example, Augustine's strategy is very revealing. He attacked Porphyry's distinction between effective rituals (theurgy) and fraudulent rituals (magic). Brushing aside any distinction between these two categories, Augustine makes his own strategic hierarchy in which all pagan practices ranked at the bottom. For Augustine, theurgy is the invention of lying demons (*City of God* 10.10).

Porphyry's rituals were no better than magic, Augustine argued, because they were vulnerable to manipulation for evil ends. As proof, Augustine referred to Porphyry's story about a Chaldean who complained that his efforts to purify souls had been thwarted by someone with greater supernatural power. "For if this business was concerned with 'good gods,' the good man who undertook to purify a soul would undoubtedly have prevailed over his malevolent opponent" (*City of God* 10.10).

47. One of the few scholars to have addressed this issue, Festugière, recognizes both Proclus' commitment to traditional gods and his "genuine" piety (1971:1581–89). Festugière tries, with only moderate success, to distinguish between theurgic operations (ἐνεργήματα) and traditional divine manifestations (ἐντυχήματα). Late Antique writers do not abide by these distinctions. Proclus connects these two types of practices, just as he combines Festugiére's "reflective piety" and "popular piety."

48. *The Liturgy of Mark* (Brightman 1965:142), English translation in Neale 1976.

49. For an English translation of the corpus and a recent bibliography, see Luibheid and Rorem 1987.

In effect, Augustine argues here that good supernatural powers should always win out over bad ones—that is, if one is good the supernatural forces of one's enemies will be less effective than one's own forces. This was a slippery position for Augustine to take, because it depends on the definitive triumph of "good"; Christian acts could be disqualified by the same reasoning. The strategy was useful, however, in his attempt to demolish Porphyry's system of classification. By introducing the invincibility of good powers, Augustine undermined the distinctions between theurgic and fraudulent rituals made by earlier writers. Every rite, or at least every pagan rite, is now simply "magic." The fantastic success of this rhetorical stance must be noted; it continues to function today in the many discussions of theurgy as a form of magic. For the Neoplatonic practitioners, this would have been nothing less than malicious slander.

Another set of debates about ritual shades into the magic versus theurgy debates, although it is cast in slightly different terms. For want of a better phrase, I call this dimension of ritual the aesthetics of ritual. Aesthetics is concerned with notions of beauty, and, I argue, rituals were evaluated in this manner. That is, in Late Antiquity different modes of interacting with supernatural figures were not all considered equally elegant and pleasing to the deity/deities. The criteria used for evaluation were again shared across what we think of as the boundaries of traditions. One common Late Antique mapping of ritual aesthetics points toward a low evaluation of or skepticism about the use of objects in ritual. For example, Origen argued that Moses used both a divine rod and a verbal formula (*logos*) so that he would not be suspected of magic, which would involve *only* a rod (*Selection on Exodus* [PG 12.284B]).

The use of props seems to have been taken as evidence that the ritual employed lower-level supernatural powers such as daimons. A rabbinic anecdote, for example, uses the two appearances of the biblical term for "magic" spelled slightly differently in arguing for the existence of two kinds of magic, one that uses props and one that does not (bSanhedrin 67b). The person who uses props is using daimons, and hence doing an inferior type of practice.

If props are evidence of baser rituals, language-only rituals were placed higher on the scale. Justin, for example, argued that the use of the name of God is better than the "incantations and incense of pagan and Jewish exorcists" (*Dialogue with Trypho* 85.3). John Chrysostom argued that Christians should rely on words, and words alone, in their rites. He implicitly acknowledges a hierarchy and tries to place Christian practice at the top. The only "praxis" employed by good Christians is making the sign of the cross (*Homilies on Collossians* 8.5 [Col 3:5).[50] Hilarion brags that the simple recitation of a name is enough, all by itself, for a healing (Weltin 1960:87). Similarly, the recitation of words alone was understood to be sufficient to transform the Eucharist (Weltin 1960: 83, 89).

Thus the very best rituals in the eyes of *some* Jews, *some* Christians, and *some* Greco-Roman practitioners would be those directed to the highest powers and employing the fewest objects. Just beyond the top of the ritual scale would be the divine person characterized by his ability to do miracles based on his indwelling power alone (M. Smith 1978:74). The claim was made that Apollonius of Tyana did not need sacrifices, prayers, or even words to perform miracles (*Philostratus Life of Apollonius* 7.38).[51]

The stance of Plotinus represents perhaps the purest form of this aesthetic snobbery, rejecting any notion of external rite at all. Some rituals were blatantly ridiculous to Plotinus, such as those that included "melodies, shrieks, whisperings and hissing with the voice" (*Enneads* 2.9.14).[52] Beyond that, he disdained prayers altogether, resulting only in "ποιήσεις/fabrications" (4.4.26).[53] Although he considered prayer déclassé, Plotinus did not deny its efficacy. The gods do answer prayers, and he can explain why: sympathy (4.4.26). Putting the cosmic forces of sympathy into play is no better than using daimons or nonsense sounds. All of this is inferior to the use of mind to commune with the deity.

50. This sign should be employed, for example, when going near a synagogue to ward off the daimons who live there (*Against the Judaizers* 8.8; 940).

51. For supernatural power without spells, see Theodoret [Pseudo-Justin] *Answer to the Orthodox* 24 and Arnobius *Against the Nations* 1.43–44.

52. Rist notes that Plotinus equated prayer with magic (1967:27). In a partisan statement, Dodds claimed that Plotinus' notion of mystical union "is attained, not by any ritual of evocation or performance of prescribed acts, but by an inward discipline of the mind which involves no compulsive element and has nothing whatever to do with magic" (1947:58). This claim repeats Plotinus' own claim to spiritual superiority, as does Majercik's characterization of Plotinus' goal as "a genuine contemplative experience free of external manipulation" (1989:39).

53. Iamblichus uses the same term in his criticisms of Egyptian sacrificial traditions (*On the Mysteries* 5.8; 208.15).

A similar notion may be behind the position of some early Christians who, Irenaeus reported, were against the use of water in rituals. "[T]he mystery of the ineffable and invisible power ought not to be performed by means of visible and corruptible created things, nor the inconceivable and incorporeal by means of what is perceptible and corporeal."[54] It is not surprising that their preferred means of redemption was using the mind to acquire special knowledge, an entirely "spiritual" endeavor.[55]

The reason for the disdain Plotinus had for much standard ritual becomes apparent in the infamous temple scene reported by his biographer. Here Plotinus permits his power to be revealed and it turns out that his indwelling supernatural power is a god and not a lowly demon. He does not need to implore other divine powers; he himself *is* one. Plotinus' rejection of prayer stems from his notion of the divine soul—to whom could he pray to except himself, and why pray to himself? The same attitude is displayed in his reply to a request to go to a religious ceremony: "It is for the gods to come to me, not for me to go to them" (Porphyry *Life of Plotinus* 10).

For Plotinus, "contemplation (θεωρεία) alone stands untouched by magic" (*Enneads* 4.4.44).[56] This appears persuasive to some modern writers, who see him as a holdout against irrational magic and ritual.[57] His goal, however, the quest for being "god-like" (1.6.9), is not rational, and neither are his methods. Plotinus may appear "rational" because he admits ignorance rather than fill in the gaps in his theoretical system by telling myths (one of the sins he attributes to the "gnostics"). He also tries to argue from principles, but that does not make him rational if the principles he argues from are irrational. Even his "philosophical" approach involves techniques. In the case of Plotinus, we find contemplation based on mental imaging of the sphere that is the world soul.[58]

54. Irenaeus *Against the Heresies* 1.21.4. See Epiphanius' account of the "Archontics," *Medicine Chest* 40.2.

55. Irenaeus denounces these individuals as "gnostics," one of the great polemical terms from Late Antiquity translated best in this context perhaps as "know-it-alls."

56. On the mental process of contemplation, see also *Enneads* 1.6. Shaw points out that scholars have long identified Plotinus' stance with Neoplatonism in general, even though he appears to be in the minority on this point (1985:3).

57. This is especially true of the classic work of E. R. Dodds.

58. *Enneads* 1.6.9 suggests "Withdraw inside yourself," followed by the analogy of making a statue. See Rappe 1995 for a discussion of Plotinus' mental imaging techniques.

When Olympius, a jealous opponent of Plotinus, sends "star spells" against him, Plotinus is able to reflect these rays back on the opponent.[59] He is successful because of his divine status, not because of some presumed rational stance of his. To see superiority in Plotinus' ability to ward off the star spells without having to actually "do" something is to adopt the aesthetic stance of Plotinus.[60]

Most Late Antique thinkers had a higher opinion of rituals. Iamblichus is a good example, because he opposed cutting oneself off from the material world. He believed that the lower and upper worlds were intimately connected and that the material world was not entirely evil. So too for Sallustius: "Prayers divorced from sacrifices are only words, prayers with sacrifices are animated words (*On the Gods* 16)," and for Albinus both contemplation (θεωρεῖα) and action (πρᾶξις) lead to divine likeness (*Introduction* 3). In all these cases the positive evaluation of ritual action may have seemed misguided to the "gnostics," who favored internalized rituals, and to Plotinus, who polemicized against any form of prayer. However, these rituals had the authority of being extremely old. They were thought to be connected with being connected with ancient sacrificial traditions and revelations from the gods.

The terms "magic" and "theurgy" are similar in that they are best understood as ways of evaluating and characterizing rituals, and not just simple references to a specific set of rituals. Anything and everything could be "magic" because the world was full of unexplained events that were threatening to someone. Seen through the lens of "theurgy," both old and new rituals spoke to a central religious concern of the Late Antique period: overcoming the gulf between humans and gods.[61] Why then coin a new term?[62] In the context of self-conscious reflection on the function of rituals about ritual that appear to have flourished in the second

59. Porphyry *Life of Plotinus* 10. For the sage's ability to ward off spells, see *Enneads* 4.4.43.

60. When Andrew Smith argues that the differences between Plotinus and Iamblichus were more semantic than substantive (1974:9), he is struggling with the same elusive issues that I call aesthetics. See the comment by Shaw (1985:7).

61. See the comments by Hirschle 1979:12ff.

62. Bidez believed the term was invented to denigrate theology and theologians, who can talk only about the gods (1965:369 n. 8), but we have no evidence that those who championed "theurgy" spurned theology.

century and later, a word was needed to parallel "theology." Just as words about the divinity are called "theology," so too now actions that involve divinity can explicitly be referred to as "theurgy." Rituals, including traditional ones, now have a label that carried with it an implied efficacy.

Whatever the original impetus for the term "theurgy," its usage varied widely. Most important, "theurgy" was used in highly strategic ways. Modern scholars should not flatten these rich usages with oversimplified characterizations of theurgy as referring to a specific, often extremely narrow set of rites. Nor should theurgic rites been seen as any more suspect than other rituals employed in these centuries.

We have found a spectrum of modes for constructing rituals: the spectrum runs from "words only" rituals that consist primarily of the recitation of verbal formulas, to rituals that combine the recitation of formulas with the use of some types of objects, and finally to rituals that do not include any verbal formulas at all. We begin analyzing this spectrum by looking at the most powerful words: at divine names.

2

THE DIVINE NAME AS EFFECTIVE LANGUAGE

In every place where I cause my name to be remembered,
I will come to you and bless you.
—Exodus 20:24

WHAT IS A DIVINE NAME?

Our investigation into effective language begins with one small but very special area of biblical interpretation: interpretation of God's name, and especially as it intersects with the notion of a special mode of divine speech. A prime locus of discussion about divine speech is exegesis of the creation story in Genesis, a story that implied to ancient readers that speech could create literal reality.[1]

The dramatic manner in which the deity's speaking is an effective and ordering force in the universe was perceived by later interpreters to be a central message of the Genesis text. In the process of discussing the creation story, the exegetes tried to capture the creativity of the deity's words and employ these pragmatics for their own ends. The particular twist that concerns us most is the emerging idea that the word(s) God spoke when creating the world was his name. Unpacking the pragmatic implications of the divine name lays bare for us the pragmatics of ritual language spoken by humans. The efficacy of words spoken by the deity will lead us to the efficacy of words spoken by humans, which in turn derive power from their divine source.

In the Hebrew Scriptures the deity has a distinct name presented as the four letters "YHWH." Since the text appears without vocalization, the

1. Numerous writers have discussed this theme. For one recent discussion that intersects with this chapter, see Tambiah 1985:17–59.

exact ancient pronunciation of the letters is not known.[2] This name distinguished him from other deities in the earliest biblical texts (e.g., Baal).
Some biblical texts imply a secret, perhaps powerful, name; just as not
everyone can see the deity, not everyone can know his name (Ex 3:14–15).
With an increasingly monotheistic vision, a name for God became redundant; because he was the only deity, he could simply be referred to as
"God."

All these biblical notions about the deity's name were extravagantly reworked and developed by Late Antique Jews and Christians. Recasting
ideas about the divine name was only one small part of the exegetical systems of nascent rabbinic Judaism and early Christianity, both of which
were founded on intricate systems of scriptural interpretation. These textual interpretations, as the exegetes themselves were aware, ranged from
defining obscure words to reading an entire text as allegory. The basic
process in all these cases was one of using language to understand, define,
and make explicit the language of the text.[3] Scriptural interpretation is full
of statements—for example, clarifying the meanings of archaic words and
giving often fanciful etymologies of names. In addition to statements
about the meanings of words, some statements are about the functions of
words.

We do not find as many statements in the Bible about the special roles
of words as we would like. For example, the efficacy of biblical blessings
and curses remains somewhat a mystery. Blessings and curses represent a
particular subgroup of verbal utterances that have an "automatic" quality about them; they cannot be taken back once spoken.[4] The reasons for
this are never explained, and we have to infer that it may be because such
utterances are understood to come directly from the deity, and therefore
stand distinct from the intention of the speaker.[5]

---

2. The name is often transliterated as "Yahweh."

3. Such words-about-words are, in the terms of linguists, metalinguistic. As Jakobson
states, "An ability to speak a given language implies an ability to talk about this language.
Such a 'metalinguistic' operation permits revision and redefinition of the vocabulary used"
(1972:162).

4. Hence the need to use euphemisms; see Mitchell 1987:160–64.

5. See Mitchell's interesting observation that for the utterance to be automatic either God
or a representative of God must be the speaker (1987:7–8, 174).

In the case of the divine name, however, we find a steady supply of statements about the role and function of that name, giving us much to analyze. The Targums, the Aramaic exegetical translations of the Hebrew Scriptures, offer many rich examples of comments, explications, and expansions of words.[6] These translations combine literal rendering of the Hebrew with various amounts of interpretative material. It is generally agreed that the Targums functioned as translations for Jews who could no longer read Hebrew. Targums were clearly also opportunities for exegetical ideas to be spun out and new meanings added to the text.

Our specific example is from *Targum Neofiti,* one of the Palestinian Targums.[7] A translation of the specific Hebrew phrases that interest us is offered here, followed by a translation of the Aramaic translation, with the additions highlighted:

Moses said to the Lord,
  "Behold, I am going to the Children of Israel and say to them, 'The God of your fathers has sent me to you,' and they will say, 'What is his name?' Who should I say sent me?"
  And the Lord said to Moses,
  "I am who I am." And he said, "And thus you will say to the children of Israel, '*I Am* sent me.'"
  (Exodus 3:14–15 [Hebrew, emphasis added])

And Moses said to the Lord,
  "Behold, I am going to the Children of Israel and say to them, 'The God of your fathers has sent me to you,' and they will say, 'What is his name?' What will I say to them?"

6. For brief introductions to the Targums, see Alexander (1990, 1992) and Flesher (1995).

7. Alejandro Diez Macho, who discovered the text in the Vatican Library, posited a first-century date. He argued (1960) that the presence of "anti-halakhic" (legal) material, inclusion of early geographical names, New Testament use of Targumic material, and disagreement with the Masoretic text are all evidence for an early (that is, pre-Christian) date. His method for dating remains controversial; more scholars posit a second- to third-century dating (York 1974; Wernberg-Moller 1962; Flesher 1995:44) or no later than the third to fourth century (Alexander 1992).

And the Lord said to Moses,

"I am who I am." And he said, "And thus you will say to the children of Israel, '*The one who spoke and the world was there at the beginning, and who is to speak to it "exist" and it will exist* sent me.'"
(*Targum Neofiti* Exodus 3:14–15 [Aramaic, emphasis added])[8]

This translation is much wordier than the original, and full of the types of
circumlocutions that occur throughout the Targums. Common among
them is the translation of "the Lord did *x*" as "the *memra* [Aramaic:
word] of the Lord did *x*." The phrase "I will be there with you" is translated, for example, "I will be there, my word, with you" (*Targum Neofiti*
Exodus 3:12). The standard explanation that *memra* is added in order to
avoid anthropomorphism fails because it is not consistent with other aspects of the translation (Klein 1972). The inclusion of "word" is in part
an extension of the biblical theme whereby God's name is a substitute for
his presence[9]—that is, the word "word" was chosen specifically to present
the divine presence as a continuation of the emerging biblical theme that
the deity is represented on earth by a substitute (an angel; a name).[10] The
theme is developed well beyond the biblical presentation and, as we shall
see, is used as a key for interpreting the biblical text itself.

The implicit claim of this translation of God's revelation of his name in
Exodus is that the new Aramaic version has the same meaning as the original Hebrew text. In the Targumic translation, however, the deity's name
is given a new characterization. If we compare the Hebrew original with
the Aramaic translation, we find that the Aramaic has expanded the deity's name from the simple "I am" to the more complex "The one who
spoke. . . ." The deity's revelation of his name to Moses is a choice opportunity for interpretation. Names present ready-made, hidden texts for
exegetes in that the semantic content of names can often be explained in a
variety of ways. Proper names logically need have no obvious semantic

8. This translation is from the edition of Diez Macho 1979.
9. See Mettinger 1982.
10. The ideology is articulated by the Deuteronomistic writers/editors. See, for example,
1 Kings 8, where "the name of the Lord," not the deity himself, is said to dwell in the earthly
Temple.

content—that is, meanings that emerge systematically from linguistic structure.[11]

It is no surprise that the exegetes chose the deity's name to embody creative speech. The notion that a name is closely linked to the person it stands for is widespread. Every name seems to be a mini-text waiting to be explained, and few exegetes can refrain from discussing names. Some biblical names are based on Hebrew roots, presenting obvious guides to exegetes in unpacking their meaning. Exegetes also supply additional meanings far beyond these roots. If names of humans properly explained reveal important information, then divine names, when properly explained, tell us about the very nature of the deity.

As modern scholars have noted, the Hebrew text of Exodus seems already to contain a short meditation on the meaning of God's name. The name usually translated as "I will be what I will be" is playing with the connection between the name YHWH (יהוה) and the root "to be (הוה)."[12] This interpretation, extended in the Aramaic translation as God's name, is expanded to reveal something essential about God's divine nature. God not only exists himself as the creator of the world; he is also the source of all existence. Thus, in order to refer to him and to explain who he is, the simplest way is to describe God in his unique role as the speaker who creates. The deity's creative act of speaking has become his proper name.

At one level this form simply tells us what the name is, just as a definition tells us the meaning of a word ("My name is *x*"). However, we already know that the meaning of the name is not limited to semantics. It is also has pragmatic implications because the deity's name is context-related speech. The definitional form therefore has an additional, less familiar, function based on its connection to the speaking situation. Divine utterances are context-related in the most extreme sense imaginable, much more so than standard examples of effective speech.

When we are aware of effective speech, as for example the binding language of a contract, this effective language usually operates in a very cir-

11. There are, of course, names such as "Hope," which do have obvious semantic content, but that is not necessary.
12. This is not to imply that the root of the name was in fact "to be," but only to state that the Exodus text appears to play with this connection. See de Vaux (1970).

cumscribed arena. The pragmatics of divine speech is distinct. The act of speaking created the world, and thereby the very possibility of speaking to the world.[13] The "creativity" of all other words and usages pales by comparison. All other creative speech is only secondary, reflected power that is dependent on the primal creative speech that established creation itself. Divine language sets the standards for the creative power of language, and the most important word in the divine language is the name of the deity.

Peircean semiotic analysis offers us a term that accounts for the specific "standing for" of the divine names. The name is not an arbitrary word chosen to stand for the deity, hence it is not a symbol. Instead, it represents the deity in the less-familiar way in which an icon "stands for" its object. Just as a line is formally linked with what it represents (it must have the exact form of a line), so too here the divine name is understood to have a formal, motivated relationship with what it represents (the deity).

God's report of his name in the Exodus translation is an exegetical key to other parts of the text. This key sheds light on a general principle of the Targums; it highlights for us the status of the entire Torah as divine reported speech. We are told that God's words function differently from human words because they are icons of divinity in all instances of divine speech. The exegetical key from the Targum highlights that God is manifest on earth, in the words of the Torah, or, to put it more concretely, in the icons of divine speech contained in the Torah scroll itself. The subjects God talks about are secondary to the fact that the Torah exists as the divine presence made manifest on earth for humans.

If we return now to the multiple additions of the word "word" to the Targums, we can now see that it is the repeated articulation of an exegetical principle about the status of the text itself. The references to "word" repeatedly draw our attention to the fact that God's words are present not just as words spoken in the past but also as reported speech in the text. Divine speech, in the objectified state of the text itself, embodies the divine presence on earth. Each time the translation focuses on God's word on earth, it tries to incorporate back into the text the implicit claim of the text, that God's words work (create) on earth. Because the deity's words are present in the Torah, the words of the text are not just any collection

13. See Silverstein 1976 and 1981.

of words, but are the "creative word" manifest in the midst of the community. The word as divine presence is manifest physically in front of them in the scrolls, scrolls that contain actual tokens (examples) of divine speech.[14] The Aramaic translation also emphasizes that the creative words used by the deity are contained in the text, literally. This in turn highlights the latent power of the text. The words by which the world was created are found in the document, along with many other examples of divine speech. Each "thus says the Lord" is an utterance of divine speech, and the text is a collection of these utterances.

At this point it is worth reflecting on what we have learned about the status of the text in the eyes of the exegetes. We have seen that holiness exists in the text because it is reported speech of a particular type, reported speech of divine language. Here the exegete, the student of God's word, learns both about what the deity says and how he talks. If people could talk like the deity, they would be able to create as well.

The translation represents a major shift in thinking with regard to the Hebrew original. The scriptural text is based on an ideology of the spoken-ness of divine language ("Thus says the Lord").[15] Divine language is manifest in the examples of God's speech and in the fact that his speech always turns out to be true. In the Targums, the focus of the translation is by necessity on a collection of written words. These written words are explicitly construed as divine words, and thus as a collection of divine words now present in their written form. It is as if the translator was saying that the words spoken by the deity also exist for the reader in a written form, and it is in that form that they are accessible currently just as they were accessible in the past in spoken form. This ideology articulates the power of the written tokens of divine speech, introducing us to the idea that words written on a piece of paper can have their own special power if they are speech of the deity. These ideas can be used in rituals, as we shall see in the next section.

14. Compare this with the widespread Neoplatonic doctrine of the "συνθήματα/tokens," which appears in *Oracles* 2.3 and 109.3 (Majercik 1989) and is discussed by Lewy 1978:190–96 and Shaw 1995: 48–50, 162. These tokens also are iconic representations.

15. Except for engraving the Ten Commandments on a stone tablet, the deity is not described as doing any writing. On the development of the idea that scriptures are the written work of Moses, see Janowitz 1991.

THE INTERPRETED NAME: A RABBINIC NAMING OF THE NAME

The link forged between the divine name and the creation story is only part of a rich complex of Jewish exegetical ideas about creative language.[16] Given the sheer breadth of rabbinic exegetical literature (third through seventh centuries), numerous and even contradictory themes on this topic appear. This section examines a few examples of the rich exegetical traditions about the divine name that place it at the center of creative language.[17]

Looking backward for a moment, the creative power of the divine name is not a biblical notion—that is, it is not explicitly stated in the biblical text that the deity's name is an automatic source of divine power.[18] The creativity of God's word is mentioned in a few scriptural references,[19] and his name is conceived as a representation of his presence.[20] There are also injunctions against the improper use of God's name, but the Scriptures contain no prohibition against merely stating it.[21] The biblical stories still present the name of the deity primarily as something he reveals in order to make himself known to the Israelites and other nations.

While the creative function of the deity's name was not biblical, the notion predates its appearance in numerous rabbinic anecdotes.[22] One of the first examples of the automatic power of the divine name is Artapanus' story that Moses uttered the name of his deity into Pharaoh's ears with the result that Pharaoh had to be brought back to life by Moses.[23] The name

16. In his survey of rabbinic literature, Idel (1992) delineates five ways in which language and creation are connected, each represented by at least one anecdote. He differentiates between (1) the Torah as the paradigm for creation, (2) human letter-combining as the mode of creating the Tabernacle, (3) God speaking divine names, (4) God speaking creative words, and (5) letters as the structural elements used in creation. Themes 2 and 5 are discussed in Chapter 4 and themes 1, 3, and 4 are covered in this section.

17. Yet another mode of creative language, heavenly liturgy, is examined in Chapter 5.

18. Scholem noted that what he called the power of the divine name was not a biblical notion (1972a:63).

19. See, for example, Ps 33:6, 9 and Sir 43:5.

20. As mentioned briefly above.

21. The closest parallels in biblical texts are blessings and curses.

22. For more discussion of this topic, see Fossum 1985:245–53, who cites many of the sources listed below, and Janowitz 1989:25–26.

23. Artapanus is usually dated to third to second century B.C.E. (Collins 1985:890–903). This particular story is preserved in both Eusebius *Preparation for the Gospel* 9.27 and Clement of Alexandria *Miscellanies* 1.23; see Collins 1985:901 and Holladay 1983:219.

is clearly understood to be a powerful word in this story, with the automatic power to kill. The setting in Artapanus points to the wider Hellenistic context. No Greco-Roman texts developed these ideas as much as the later Jewish texts, and particularly rabbinic texts.

The *Book of Jubilees* 36:7[24] and the *Prayer of Manasseh* 1:3[25] both refer to an oath that contains the divine name that was used in the creation of the world. These examples are significant because they connect the divine name with creation and because this theme reappears in numerous rabbinic anecdotes.[26] They are limited, however, in that the power of the name may derive in part from the status of the utterance as an oath.

The link implicit in the Targums between the divine name and the act of creation is more explicit in numerous rabbinic elaborations about the power of the divine name. Disparate stories about God's name, coming from various rabbinic texts edited over hundreds of years, are all united in their semiotic mode of presentation of the name. The iconic status of the divine name is established and embellished in numerous exegetical texts that recount its unique function and inherent power. Some stories explore its power, and hence the need to limit drastically its use, and even its mention. A particularly rich anecdote states that the deity's name was not supposed to be uttered in court by a witness to blasphemy (mSanhedrin 7:5)—that is, even in the highly defined setting of a witness report the name cannot be uttered, because it is impossible to separate out the reporting of the deity's name from its use.

Others ask about the definitional limits of the name (What is the name? Is there only one?). As for the definitional limits of the name, some would extend punishment for blasphemy even to those who substituted divine attributes for the divine name (bSanhedrin 56a). This ideology endows the attributes with the same status as the divine name itself. So too the letters of the divine name are as powerful as the name; a midrashic text discusses

24. The *Book of Jubilees* is usually dated to the first century B.C.E.

25. This text is usually dated to the second to first centuries B.C.E.; see Charlesworth 1985:627.

26. See bSuccah 53a, jSanhedrin 10:2, bMaccot 11a, *Targum Pseudo-Jonathan* to Exod 28:30, bSanhedrin 29a, and *Midrash Samuel* 26. *Odes of Solomon* 4:7–8 mentions a seal but does not refer directly to the divine name. In midrashic texts the abyss is sealed with the Torah; see Sperber 1966:173.

the destruction of the world by two letters from the divine name (*Genesis Rabba* 12.10).[27]

The power of the divine name was harnessed by select biblical figures who used it for protection and even for violent acts of aggression. Solomon uses a ring with the divine name on it to subdue a demon (bGittin 68b); Moses kills an Egyptian with the divine name (*Exodus Rabba* on 1.29). The divine name could animate lifeless images and statutes, a notion that was later to be popularized with the story of the golem.[28] Entire histories of the divine name or, rather, a series of conflicting histories were composed by the rabbinic exegetes. The distant past and the future were both portrayed as times when people knew (or would know) how to use the divine name, as the knowledge of the name became a metaphor for the presence of the deity on earth and for his interaction with his people. For example, one anecdote states that the divine name was once entrusted to the entire nation of Israelites, given to them during their journey through the desert. It was taken away, however, because of the Israelites' worship of the Golden Calf.[29] Perhaps the most famous "history" is that although at one time the name was widely known, growing corruption led to increasing restrictions until the name was not used anymore.[30]

Once this interpretation of the divine name had been developed, the name was itself "named." The name was given a name as a shorthand reference that both included a reference to the fact that it is a name and referred to its complex content. The divine name is now named the "Meforash/Explicit Name (שם המפורש)" based on the root "פרש/explain, make explicit."[31] Even though the root is commonly used to refer to the process of interpreting and explicating, the Explicit Name is restricted in its use. Already in 1901, Max Gruenbaum argued that this phrase had connotations of secrecy (Gruenbaum 1901:244). He noted the similar us-

27. See bMenahot 29b; *Genesis Rabba* 1:10; 3 Enoch 13.1; Masseket Hekalot, Jellenik, Bet Ha-Midrash, 2.46. See also Alexander 1983b:265 and Fossum 1985:253–55.

28. In bSota 47a and bSanhedrin 107b, Gechazi animates Jeroboam's calves by placing the divine name in their mouths, and they begin to speak.

29. *Song of Songs Rabba* 1:2, 5:1, 8:1 (on Exod 33:6) recounts two theories about the divine name, one that the name erased itself, and the other that an angel descended and erased it.

30. See bYoma 39b; jYoma 3.7. This explains why prayers are no longer effective (*Midrash on Psalms* 91:8).

age of the root in the Targumic translation of Judges 13:18. In the Hebrew text, an angel refuses to tell Manoach his name because it is "wondrous (פלאי)"; in the Aramaic translation, the name is described as "Meforash."

Unfortunately the appearance of the doctrine about the Explicit Name is very difficult to date. Scholem stated that "Meforash," connoting "secret," appeared "from the 2nd or 3rd century onwards," but he did not go into any more detailed discussion of the topic (1972a:68). The Hebrew texts in which the term appears are all difficult to date, and we lack clear parallels to help us with a more precise dating.

It is tempting, but wrong, to guess exactly which name this name-for-the-name refers to. As a name for the divine name, the term cannot be explained by pinpointing a unique name to which it refers. The term crystallizes in a single unit the ideas discussed so far—that is, the term signals that a secret, powerful name exists, a name that itself is an object of speculation and investigation.

Not only is the divine name a text to be studied, but it is also a powerful text. The term "Explicit Name" is a shorthand reference for the process of divine naming, both as the name refers to the deity and as it is an instrument of creativity. Exegesis of the Divine Name is exegesis of all the deity's power bundled in a single word. The choice of name is simple, again because "name" most closely "stands for" the deity.

With the "Explicit Name," we arrive at the heart of the rabbinic ideology of ritual language.[32] According to rabbinic tradition the Name can be uttered only once a year by the High Priest when he is in the Holy of Holies on Yom Kippur—that is, it can be spoken only by the holiest person at the holiest time of year in the holiest place. All rabbinic blessing formulas ("Blessed are you, Adonai") are built around the recitation of a divine name that, while it is not the "Explicit Name," is a highly restricted and powerful divine name that derives from the Explicit Name.

The iconicity of the divine name is seen in the focus on form as an in-

---

31. Classic discussions of the Explicit Name include Bacher (1901), Gruenbaum (1901), Marmorstein (1927), and Cohon (1951). This name is contrasted with the nickname in bSota 38a.

32. This is also the heart of their theory of textuality as seen in the additions of the word "word" in the Targums.

tegral aspect of the name. The structure of the object (deity) is revealed in the structure of the word (name/text). The shape of the written form must be preserved exactly, because it is part of the significance of the name, hence the emphasis on the shape of the letters in copying the name.[33] The scriptural text derives its value to the extent that it is a copy of this pattern. An analogy has been established between name and text; simply put, because the name can be a text, a text can be a name.[34] Just as the Torah is said to have existed before creation, so too did the divine name, as the Torah and the name become two mirroring versions of the primordial text.[35]

The extremely dramatic relationship of the text to its context is played out in the anecdote that the addition or subtraction of a single letter will destroy the world.[36] This anecdote is also a clear indication of the name's iconic power. Other stories recount the necessity of rearranging the manifest content in order to find the content that must be hidden due to its potential use and misuse. If the correct order had been given, anyone could use it to wake the dead or perform miracles (*Midrash on Psalms* 3.2). Synagogues are in turn holy places because they house these divine manifestations.[37] The name is literally manifested in the scroll, which becomes a written incarnation. The meaning of the text is no longer limited to the semantic meaning of the words it contains.[38]

Because God created the world by speaking his name, this "washes

33. This emphasis on the form led to preserving the Hebrew letters even in Greek translations, where they would be read backward.

34. In the thirteenth century Nachmanides stated, "We possess an authentic tradition showing that the entire Torah consists of the names of God and that the words we read can be divided in a very different way, so as to form names" (*Commentary on Bereshit* 1:1). He cites the image of black fire on white fire as proof that the Torah can be read either in the traditional manner or as a series of names. The black fire on white fire image is found in *Midrash Konen*, Jellenik, Bet Ha-Midrash 2.23–24. See Idel 1981.

35. *Pirkei de R. Eliezer*, chap. 3. cited by Scholem 1972a:70. Idel's theme 1 (see note 16 above), Torah as paradigm of creation, posits that the world as we know it is a copy of a written text. This is a bold attempt to give priority to text, and it also fits in with the shift from spoken divine language to written divine language outlined above.

36. Attributed to Rabbi Ishmael in bErubin 13a. See Scholem 1965a:39.

37. See the brief comment by Lightstone 1984:118 on the scrolls as holy "relics."

38. In linguistic terms, the name becomes less and less semantic as it is encoded in the text into a calibrated, hyperstructured type of discourse that is at basis metapragmatic.

out" the semantic content of the divine utterances in Genesis 1—that is, the content of the creative speech act in Genesis is not limited to the uttering of "Let there be light" and so on. Divine speech is not primarily *about* anything so much as it is the example par excellence of God's creative power (in our terms, not primarily semantic, but pragmatic).

This stunningly complex ideology of the divine name will reappear in still later Jewish texts and will continue for centuries to make both writing and speaking the divine name subject to extensive taboos. To unsympathetic outsiders, the divine name will suffer the same fate as "voodoo," and that which is most holy will be held up by outsiders as the model of the lowest forms of ritual practice. However, to those who understand the pragmatic implications of using the divine name, numerous rituals will begin to make sense.

3
Thinking with the Divine Name:
Theories of Language in
Christian Exegesis

> My reverence, Protarchus, for the names of the gods is profound.
> —Plato *Philebus* 12C, cited twice by Origen
> (*Against Celsus* 1.25, 4.48)

Christian exegesis paralleled Jewish explication of the divine name and its role in creation. At the same time, Christian exegesis developed its own distinct theories.[1] *First Clement,* for example, claims: "Your name is the primal source of all creation" (61.59.2). In this chapter we consider two Christian writers—Origen (third century) and Dionysius the Areopagite (fifth century)—both of whom wrote specifically about divine names. Origen, who had close ties to Jewish exegetes, shares many of the same ideas we found in the rabbinic anecdotes.[2] For example, in his commentary on the Song of Songs (*Homilies on the Song of Songs* 1.6) and in *Against Celsus* (4.34) he attributes the interpretation of divine names to "Hebrews."[3] As de Lange has pointed out (1976:118), the term "שמות דורש/name interpreter" attributed to Rabbi Meir and Rabbi Joshua ben Qorlah (*Ruth Rabba* 2.5 and *Genesis Rabba* 42.5) is similar to Origen's term "interpretes nominum." Origen's discussion, however, is not limited to anecdotes, for he outlines some of the philosophical ideas behind the power of names. As such, and because it is pos-

---

1. Fossum discusses similar Samaritan texts (1985:76ff., 97ff.).

2. For discussion of Origen's contact with Jews, see G. Bardy 1937:221–23, Gögler 1963, N. de Lange 1976, H. Bietenhard 1974, David Halperin 1980, and Paul Blowers 1988. Bardy lists sixty-nine examples of traditions he believes Origen borrowed from Jews. Bietenhard cites more than forty examples, most of them also cited by Bardy, and includes specific citations from Hebrew exegetical writings for most of his examples. Origen's particular amalgam of ideas about names was influenced, as he states, by the ideas of Hebrew name interpreters.

3. See *Homilies on Exodus* 5.1 and *Homilies on Genesis* 12.4.

sible to date his writings much more specifically, his presentation is particularly valuable when it intersects with and expands on the Jewish anecdotes discussed in the preceding chapter.

Dionysius the Areopagite, a fifth-century Christian theologian, offers a slightly modified theory of divine name;[4] such names encode in themselves specific manifestations of the deity. He rejects the notion that divine names represent the deity iconically, which is familiar from Origen, but elaborates his own version of a special connection between a divine name and the deity. For him as well, divine names are far from arbitrary. He also incorporates some striking Greco-Roman ideas about divine names, which gives us the opportunity to briefly return us to some of the Neoplatonic thinkers discussed in Chapter 1.

For all these writers, regardless of their primary religious tradition, divine names are not completely arbitrary. The names, based on different theories of their specific modes of "standing" for divinity, can be used in a variety of ritual transformations.

DIVINE NAMES IN ORIGEN

Origen mentioned divine names in a number of places,[5] but he goes into greatest detail in his *Against Celsus* where he defends against the attack by the pagan Celsus that Christians practice magic. Origen's answer to this charge is that Celsus fails to understand the true philosophy of names. Language is not of human origin, and names are not arbitrary. Using Jesus' names to heal is a practice attested to by Jesus himself, as Origen can attest from the New Testament.

He broaches the topic of language and of names in particular by mentioning and rejecting various philosophical options (*Against Celsus* 1.24). He criticizes first Aristotle's theory that there is no inherent relationship between a word and what it represents. Aristotle's influential theory dis-

---

4. For an introduction to Dionysius the Areopagite and a complete English translation of his writings, see Luibheid and Rorem 1987.

5. Origen discusses the significance of names in *Selections on Genesis* 17.5; *Homilies on Numbers* 25.3, 27.5, and 27.13; and *Homilies on Joshua* 13.2 and 13.4.

tinguished between the culturally varying words used to describe common, even universal experiences. As Parmentier explains, "For Aristotle (*De Interpretatione* 16.1), mental experiences are direct images of things all men experience uniformly, while spoken words are variable symbols of these universal images" (1985:360).[6] Origen rejects this theory because it negates any possible divine dimension of language and makes it a social construct. Equally weak, according to Origen, is the Stoic theory of "first utterances being imitations of the things described and becoming their names." Although at first blush the materialistic bent of the Stoic theories might seem closer to his, their ideas about the way words are "imitations" of objects does not permit a divine origin for language. The Epicurean argument of social conventions based on emotional reactions to objects, which Origen also rejects, must have seemed ludicrous and outrageous to him.

Particularly worrisome to Origen was Celsus' articulation of the common trope that the diverse divine names used by humans all refer to the same deity.[7] According to Origen, this argument was planted by daimons, who "attribute their own names to the supreme God so that they may be worshiped as the supreme God" (*Exhortation to Martyrdom* 46). The special power of names makes Origen hesitant even to discuss the issue. The nature of names, he writes, "is a profound and obscure question," as well as "a certain, mysterious divine science." Indeed, it is a "consistent system which has principles known to a very few" (*Against Celsus* 1.25). Names point to the deepest meanings of objects, signifying their nature and revealing their essence (*On Prayer* 24.2).

Origen finds proof of the nonarbitrariness of names in the success individuals have in summoning supernatural forces—why else do they respond to humans? Angel names, for example, are based on the activities that God gave them to do and that they may do for humans (*Against Celsus* 1.25).[8] So too, in a rabbinic exegesis of Judges 13:18, an angel replies

6. Note the presupposed transparency of his system, with different words being simply different names for the same things. Origen's remark does not go into any detail about Aristotle.

7. See *Against Celsus* 5.41, 8.69 and note 21 below.

8. See *On First Principles* 1.8.1, *Homilies on Joshua* 23.4, *Homilies on Numbers* 14.2.

to a request for his name with "I am not able to tell you my name, for the Holy One, Blessed be He, gives us a name to accord with the errand on which he sends us" (*Numbers Rabba* 10.5).

The category of divine names, as we saw in the Jewish exegesis, includes many different names. The Late Antique cosmos was populated by many types of divine characters, enlarging the pool of potential effective names. Origen casts a wide net that included names of all kinds of divine beings. "Jesus," of course, is an efficacious and divine name (*Against Celsus* 1.67). Names of patriarchs are efficacious because the patriarchs each have a divine character (4.34).[9] The name "Sabaoth" derives its meaning from the divine beings called "Sabai," with "Sabaoth" being their ruler, and Ephesians 1:21 is evidence that there are other divine beings whose names are not known (*Commentary on John* 1.34). According to Celsus, Christians, among others, can achieve special powers by employing all these names, including the names of daimons (*Against Celsus* 1.6).[10] Origen counters that Christians use only Jesus' name.

The power of a divine name is automatic and not based on the intention of the speaker, a theme that is familiar to us by now.[11] Moses knew enough about these "secret doctrines" to prohibit mentioning the names of gods, according to Origen's reading of Exodus 23:13 (*Against Celsus* 5.46). Thus, for Origen, a Christian must be careful not to speak these names of other heavenly powers, for the power would still be turned on. A Christian would rather face death than utter the word "Zeus," which, whether he meant it or not, might produce miracles (4.33–34). While Zeus may not be God, he might be a powerful daimon, and therefore an active threat.[12]

Part of the power Scripture has over humans, and its ability to influence them toward good and away from evil, is due to the automatically effective names it includes. In his *Homilies on Joshua*, Origen states that

9. The angelic status of the patriarchs was a common theme in Jewish texts found, among other places, in Philo and the Prayer of Joseph.

10. See *Against Celsus* 6.40 and *Homilies on Joshua* 20.1.

11. This is contrary to predominant features of present-day theories of language, where intentional models often supplement semantic models.

12. For similar Christian prohibitions against uttering divine names, see Tertullian's discussion in *On Idolatry* 20–21 and *Teachings of the Apostles* 21.

"more powerful than any incantation is the naming of names" (20.1).[13] The phrase from Psalm 102:1, "Praise the Lord, my soul, and let all the things within me praise his holy name," means that things (that is, powers) inside a person benefit from hearing the Scriptures read, regardless of the intention of the hearer.

Some of the power of names comes from the special qualities of Hebrew, which for Origen is the original language.[14] Names, and the prayers that contain them, lose their efficacy in translation. For example, the phrase "God of Abraham" translated as "God of the chosen father of the echo" will have no effect,[15] as Origen explains: "In this case the recitation would have no effect, as it would be no different from the names which have no power at all" (*Against Celsus* 5.45). The words must be said in Hebrew or they will be "weak and ineffective" (1.25).[16]

Because of the problems translation presents, Origen decides it must be "the qualities and characteristics of the sounds' (*Against Celsus* 1.25) that give names power.[17] While he does not use the term "icon," he understands that the semantic reference of a name is not what is important. The iconic aspects of the name would be lost in translation to other languages, because in another language a word does not have the same form.[18] Origen does not explicitly state, as the rabbis do, that the power of the sounds comes from the fact that they are the sounds of the word used to create the world. However, his interpretation of the prologue of the Gospel of John develops a Christian parallel to the Jewish theories. "In the Beginning was the Word" (John 1:1) establishes the creative "word" as neither "Let there be light" nor the divine name, but instead the Greek word "λόγος /word." Origen comments on this text: "Because he regards Him as the Creator of all things, he gives him the name of 'the word.'"

13. Translations are adapted from Dillon 1985:214–15.

14. Adam spoke Hebrew, which is proof that it the original language (*Homilies on Numbers* 11.4).

15. The reason Origen translated the name "Abraham" in this fashion is not clear. "Av" means father, but his choice of "echo" is mysterious.

16. See also *Against Celsus* 8.37.

17. The power of sounds is discussed at length in the next chapter. Neither Chadwick (1965) nor Dillon (1985) considers possible Jewish influences on this aspect of Origen's thought.

18. Compare Dillon's discussion of sense and reference, 1985:214.

Again we find a package of ideas about creative language and divine
names that is as dense and complex as the Targumic renaming. Here Jesus
as the "logos" stands for the deity in his creative aspect. How then, we
wonder with Origen, does Jesus "stand for" the deity? How does his
name, "Word," represent deity? Origen's major divergence from the
stance of the Hebrew name interpreters is that those interpreters elevated
Hebrew as the scriptural language while he dealt with Greek scriptures.[19]
Origen leaves us with the question of how the Greek word for "word"
stands for the deity.[20]

Dionysius investigates this very question, and in his answer the special
role of Hebrew is gone. The manner in which names, including the name
"Word," stand for God was as complicated as the manner in which the
material world reflects the transcendent deity. The question was the subject of a lengthy treatise by Dionysius entitled *Divine Names,* which he began with an ironic comment about his ability to reach his goal through a
discussion of the divine names. The "utterly transcendent" that he was
seeking, "it is gathered up by no discourse, by no intuition, by no name"
(*Divine Names* 1.1 588B). The idea that God was beyond any name was
by then quite old.[21]

The same point occurs later in the treatise where Dionysius cites the famous story from Judges 13:18 where an angel, asked his name, rebukes
the questioner: "Why do you ask my name, seeing it is wonderful?" (*Divine Names* 1.6 596A). For Dionysius, the rebuke means that God is so
wonderful he does not, in truth, *have* a name. "Theologians praise it by
every name—and as the Nameless One" (1.6 596A). God's name is won-

19. A similar problem was faced by Philo, who exegeted a Greek translation. He therefore developed the story of the inspired translators in order to establish the divine status of
the translation. See Janowitz 1991.

20. For Augustine's explication of a theory of how words stand for objects, see Janowitz
1991.

21. On the theme of God being beyond names, see "God has many names" (Pseudo-Aris-
totle *On the World* 7); "No name is properly used of me" (Philo *Life of Moses* 1.75); "God
needs no name" (*On Abraham* 51); "We rely on names for the nameless" (Maximus of Tyre
8:10); "Who is greater than any name" (*Corpus Hermeticum* 5.1); "Anyone who dares to
say there is a name raves" (Justin *First Apology* 61.11); "No one can utter the name of ineffable God" (*First Apology* 63.1); "No name given" (Justin *Second Apology* 6.1); "God's
name was not sent into the world" (*Martyrdom of Isaiah* 1:7). See also Josephus *Against
Apion* 2:167. See Marmorstein 1927:111.

derful—that is, above every name to such an extent that he is nameless.[22] For the Targumic translators discussed above, the root used to translate "wonderful" is the same root that serves as the root of the "Explicit Name." Their understanding of the rebuke is: Do not ask my name because it is too powerful and too secret to utter aloud.

If the deity is beyond names, why write an entire treatise called *Divine Names?* The answer is that names are actually not entirely arbitrary. A major problem in Dionysius' cosmology is how to conceive of the relationship between the highest, transcendent level and the lowest level, the world of matter. In what we could call an "emanationist" theory of language, the answer to this problem is supplied by the model of divine names. The divine names articulate the specific relationship between the lower levels (physical sounds/world) and the highest deity (what the sounds represent), calibrating the cosmos.

In this system of cosmic emanations, while at one level of understanding God is thought to be beyond names, divine names still supply crucial evidence about the deity. In part this crucial evidence is at the level of semantic meaning. Thus the *Divine Names* of Dionysius explains the meaning of each of the deity's names, starting with Good and Light. Each name, as he now demonstrates at great length, is a mini-text that reveals the deity's relationship to the world and explains his nature. As we read the lengthy treatise, which explains one name after another, we must grasp not the particular content of each name he discusses, but instead the connection between each divine name and the divinity named. In fact, for Dionysius, exegesis of the revealed names, combined with the cosmological picture developed in the other treatises, is enough to understand the entire world, all the way from the far-off God to the lowest level of matter. Dionysius wrote systematically, and in each of his four extant treatises he attacked a distinct philosophical issue. Each treatise examines a different layer of the standard Late Antique multilayered cosmology. As I. P. Sheldon-Williams notes (1972), in the treatise the *Most Mysterious Theology* Dionysius deals with God as transcendent, and in the *Celestial Hierarchy* and the *Ecclesiastical Hierarchy* he deals with the heavenly and

---

22. This theory is reminiscent of Celsus' position discussed above.

earthly orders. In *Divine Names,* he writes about "God as First Cause" (1972:68).

The linguistic unit "name," as noted above, offers a particularly rich exegetical opportunity for Dionysius to use in spinning his emanationist theory. He exploits the very specific linguistic role of "name." In the case of the attributes he discusses, all have semantic content, such as "good." Names, as we have noted repeatedly, primarily have reference—that is, they refer to the deity named. Thus they all point directly to the deity's being. For Dionysius, "God" is not his name, and anyone who confuses the name of God with God himself is obviously misguided (and magical). However, God in fact *is* his name, because each name is a manifestation, or a revelation, of the higher levels of reality now available on earth. Therefore, divine names are a striking exception to Dionysius' symbolic theory of language, according to which most words are arbitrary.

The most idiosyncratic description that concretizes this point is the statement of Dionysius that divine names are "statues." At the start of chapter 9, he writes: "Greatness and smallness, sameness and difference, similarity and dissimilarity, rest and motion—we must examine also all that is manifested to us from these statues that are divine names" (*Divine Names* 9.1 909B).[23] For him divine names "stand for" the deity in the same complex ways statues do. He is trying here to point to the kind of "standing for" relationship that Peirce calls iconic. This is another iconic theory of divine names. A statue is not identical to the deity it represents, but it is not arbitrarily depicted either. Just as a statue can be a formal representation of divinity, so too can a divine name be a representation of divinity too.

This striking linguistic theory, that divine names are statues, is found scattered throughout the writings of Proclus, whom we encountered above. Dionysius was greatly indebted to Proclus and borrowed many philosophical ideas from him.[24] Proclus' theory of divine names was part of his general theory of language, articulated in his commentaries on

23. Luibhied translates this phrase "divinely named images" (1987:115).

24. Proclus probably did not invent the notion of divine names as statues of God, but it appears that he popularized it. Its absence in Iamblichus and Julian points to the early fifth-century Athens, when Syrianus and Plutarch of Athens were teaching there (Saffrey 1982:70).

Plato.[25] Language, while it is essentially human, is not based on chance, but instead manifests the essences of things. Proclus' additional refinement of these common ideas is the parallel he draws between the act of naming and intellectual knowledge; beings higher up on the scale have greater capacity for both. Humans can demonstrate their divine knowledge when they give names to objects, because the process of naming is participation in divine power (*Commentary on the Cratylus* 42, p. 13.19–27) and intellectual activity. "There are many grades of names, as of knowledge. . . . And some are names we too can utter, others are explicit. In short, as the Cratylus has taught us and before it divinely inspired tradition, both knowledge and name-giving among the gods transcends ours" (*Commentary on the Parmenides* p. 853.1–3). Just as a divine presence illuminates a statue in a ritual, so too the human mind, when it expresses a divine name in 'articulated sounds' reveals the hidden being of the gods" (*Platonic Theology* 1.29.123–24).[26]

This theory has implications for rituals; it motivates the use of names and the sounds of names in rituals. Thus in Proclus' rituals, referred to as theurgy, the officiant may speak incomprehensible sounds that are in fact divine names. These sounds are "natural" and not based on social convention, and are therefore directly connected to the supernatural world.

Dionysius not only shares Proclus' extremely distinctive "names are statues" definition, but also uses the word "theurgy" to describe the Eucharist.[27] In one of his letters, he writes that Jesus passed on not only parables but also "the mysterious rites of theurgy through the symbolism of a table" (Letter 9.1 1108A).[28] Dionysius is therefore able, through this rite, to manifest heavenly workings on earth, to connect the many layers of the cosmos, and to demonstrate the uppermost secrets in the earthly "symbols" of the bread and the wine by their transformation.

The bread and the wine are representations of divine power in the same way that divine names are "statues," though the manifestation of heav-

25. Proclus' most extensive discussion of language is in his *Commentary on the Cratylus* 71, pp. 29–35). See Trouillard 1975.

26. For other references to names as statues, see his *Commentary on the Cratylus* 51, pp. 18.27–19.17 and *Commentary on the Parmenides*, p. 851, 8–10.

27. See Chapter 1 for an extended discussion of the term "theurgy."

28. Luibhied translates this as "mysteries of his divine activity" (1987:283).

enly workings in the Eucharist is more dramatic and more directly efficacious than that of divine names. Even the teachings of the saints are called
"theurgical lights," also revealing divine power on earth for individuals
who can read the teachings correctly (*Divine Names* 1.4 592B).

Translation from one language to another is not a problem for either
Proclus or Dionysius. Proclus states that the divine names of the Egyptians, the Chaldeans, the Indians, and the Greeks all have their own efficacy.[29] The "grounding" of effective language is based on the universal
relationship of divinity to world, which has an international status and
transcends any particular language.

At first glance, the theory of Dionysius is best described, in Peircean
terms, as symbolic and not iconic. Dionysius will state mockingly, "Is it
wrong to call twice times two four?"[30] on the basis that they are simply
two different names for the same thing. If Dionysius does not explicitly label Origen's strange-sounding Hebrew names with their innate power as
"magical," someone with his point of view will sooner (Celsus) or later
(Dillon 1985) make that exact assessment.

At the same time, Dionysius will argue that names are specific manifestations of divine power on earth and that language has a transformational role in rituals. He will, for example, never say that a priest can say
whatever he wants over the Eucharist, for the transformation at the Eucharist is dependent on having the exact formula spoken over the bread
and the wine.

Moreover, the words and the "symbols" of the Eucharist are transformational. Dionysius repeatedly states that the Christian rituals "divinize,"
showing that the object of the rite is the transformation of not only the
bread and the wine but also the participants. In a statement that is shock-
ing by modern standards, he claims: "Sacred deification occurs in him directly from God" (*Ecclesiastical Hierarchy* 2.1).[31] Thus Saffrey translates

29. *Commentary on the Cratylus* 71, p. 32. Proclus also writes here that the amount of
power unleashed depends on the status of the divine being who is invoked, a point reminiscent of Origen.

30. Dionysius employs this argument to support his exegesis (*Divine Names* 4.11 708C).
The meaning of the text can be represented by either the text or its exegesis.

31. Thus Luibhied translates "theurgy" as "God's works," a switch from objective to
subjective genitive (1987).

Dionysius' use of "theurgy" as "the mysteries by which one is made a god" (1982:72). By explaining to us his theory of names and his most secret theology, Dionysius provides us with model for manipulating and transforming earthly elements to reveal divine ones. His use of language may be more familiar to us, perhaps, than Origen's, but in the end divine names are still formal representations of divinity on earth. Language is no less transformational than for Origen, and can manifest heavenly elements from earthly.

4

THE MEANING OF LETTERS: FROM DIVINE NAME TO COSMIC SOUNDS

We use not just words, but sounds full of efficacy.
—*Corpus Hermeticum* 16.2

T he use of letters in rituals is not a simple or obvious topic. The notion that letters, which have no meanings, have cultural functions
is even stranger perhaps than the idea that words do. Analyzing
divine names, however, has prepared us for this idea, because names do
not always have meaning (semantics). It is a small step from divine names
to the letters and sounds of those names.

For this chapter, the first example of the meaning of sounds is a divine
revelation about the creation of the world attributed to the second-
century Christian thinker Marcus. The revelation about the origin of the
cosmos turns out to be a complex narrative about language, with names,
words, letters, and sounds being the vehicles of and models for creation.
Marcus' narrative explains how the divine name created the world, and in
that process he reworks standard distinctions between words and letters.
That reworking provides us with numerous models for the meanings of
letters, many of which were probably of Jewish origin.

For Marcus, divine speech makes accessible for humans that which is
unspeakable (divine). At the same time, as in the Targum example, divine
language is not primarily language *about* anything (semantics) and therefore may not be easily comprehensible to humans. The nonsemantic dimensions of language reveal subtler and deeper information about reality
and divinity if properly understood—that is, if the way in which letters are
signs is understood. Divine language literally embodies all the characteristics of divinity, as confusing as that may be to humans. The sounds of letters are heightened language because they are cosmic sounds linked to the
structure of the divine realm.

Marcus' discussion offers a point of departure for examining in turn a Hebrew text about letters, the *Book of Creation* (*Sefer Yetsira*), a dense meditation on the pragmatics of letters. The text is a barely comprehensible investigation into the linguistic processes by which the world was made. The distinction between speculative and ritual texts is blurred, because the speculation is about inherently powerful letters. Finally, we shall turn to some Neoplatonic texts that offer additional theoretical grounding for the pragmatics of letter sounds.

Marcus' ideas are presented at length, and roundly denounced, by his opponent Irenaeus (c. 130–c. 200 C.E.), who viewed Marcus as a heretic and threat to Christianity.[1] The presentation is somewhat cryptic, probably due to its inherent complexity and not to any distortions introduced by Irenaeus. Marcus claimed to have had a unique revelation from a heavenly figure who told him the "origin of all things, which it has never revealed to any one either of gods or men." This claim to secret knowledge appears to have annoyed Irenaeus tremendously.

The model for creation is speech that takes the ineffable and makes it effable. The female revelatory figure begins by telling Marcus that God created the world by manifesting himself in the pronunciation of his name. "When first the unoriginated, inconceivable Father willed to bring forth that which is ineffable in him, and to endow with form that which is invisible, he opened his mouth, and sent forth the Word similar to himself who standing near, showed him what he himself was" (*Against the Heresies* 1.14.1).

Jewish influence on this text, which is based on a four-letter divine name mentioned shortly after this introduction, has long been noted.[2] The Christian version secures the dating of this influence. The particular and by now familiar twist here is that the deity created the world by a "Word" which is "similar to himself." He could then see this linguistic unit, which had the same form as he did. This is a clear description of a Peircean icon. While it is difficult to think of a word as being visible, this one is specifically said to be.

---

1. Irenaeus *Against the Heresies* 1.13–22 (paralleled in Epiphanius *Against the Heresies* 34.4.1–7 and followed in Hippolytus *Refutation of All Heresies* 6.37). Translations of Irenaeus are taken from Roberts and Donaldson 1979, with slight modifications. For discussions of Marcus, see Dornseiff 1922:126–33 and Morray-Jones 1993.

2. Gaster 1971, 2:130–35, Dornseiff 1922:126–32.

The revelation that follows presents a number of specific models of the primordial utterance, and its exact role in creation. The first model is of a single word splitting into many pieces, which explains the complexity of the material world. Just as in the example from the Targums, the divine name becomes a complex of many "words," in this case four words of 30 letters (4 + 4 + 10 + 12).[3] With so many segments, the extended name comes to include all the letters of the alphabet. The words forget their unitary origin, each thinking that it is the whole sound.

The old Latin translator of Irenaeus understood the word "beginning" from the phrase "which was the beginning" not as a temporal marker, but as the first word spoken and then referred back to in the next phrase ("and that utterance consisted of four letters"). He therefore preserved the Greek word for "beginning" untranslated in his Latin text, as if he sensed that part of the meaning of the word was its exact form.[4]

Marcus' second model posits that humans can find the form and content of the creative name in unexpected places. The "emblem of this utterance"—that is, of the reunited sounds, is the word "amen" (*Against the Heresies* 1.14.8). "Amen" has no simple meaning; it marks the assent of the audience to the praise offered. In this model, the word is yet another icon of cosmic sound. Thus far in the text a number of linguistic units function as icons (name, beginning, the four words, amen), but none of these linguistic units is intended to function primarily for communication; other nonsemantic linguistic units can function similarly. According to Marcus, the cry of the infant leaving the womb "is in accordance with the sound of every one of these elements," an image based on "Out of the mouth of babes and infants you have perfected praise" (Ps 8:2). So too when "The heavens declare the glory of God" (Ps 19:1), also cited by Marcus, the heavens do not necessarily speak in simple declarative sentences. These emblems are the sounds that "remain below as if cast outside" when the letters ascend back up to the heavenly world. The sounds

3. We are never told the specific four words that were uttered first. The four-letter names point to a Hebrew original, and perhaps the four words are not included because they did not translate well from a Hebrew original to the Greek version.

4. The Hebrew name for the deity was sometimes preserved untranslated in Greek texts, leading to great confusion among later readers.

of letters are still available to humans even after the bodies, which make letters manifest in the lower world, return to their origin.

The third model Marcus offers is familiar from Jewish sources as well, and adds a fourth dimension to any text: all the hidden words manifest only by their first letters. The letter "delta," for example, is itself a word that can be broken down into the name for each letter: delta, epsilon, lambda, and so on.[5] Once this happens, the difference between words and letters collapses. Each word (name) is made up of letters, which are themselves revealed to be words made up of letters. These hidden words mirror the complexity of the cosmos, which, as we saw, stems from the many different sounds generated from the primordial word(s). Here the distinction between word and letter dissolves, and we see how a single word generates multiple other words.

Marcus' fourth model is the part of his revelation cited most often, the description of a female "Body of Truth." "Behold, then, her head on high, Alpha and Omega; her neck, Beta and Psi; her shoulders with her hands, Gamma and Chi; her breast, Delta and Phi, her diaphragm, Epsilon and Upsilon; her back, Zeta and Tau; her belly, Eta and Sigma; her thighs, Theta and Rho; her knees, Iota and Pi; her legs, Kappa and Omicron; her ankles, Lambda and Xi; her feet Mu and Nu" (*Against the Heresies* 1.14.3). The giant female figure incarnates divinity simultaneously in a human-like body and in letters. This description is a fascinating nuance on the trope, familiar from the Hebrew Scriptures, of describing the deity and other heavenly beings as having human-like bodies. Some Jews view this practice with skepticism or reject it outright as being an unacceptable mode of thinking about divinity. In fact, the anti-anthropomorphic stance has been so influential that it is sometimes difficult for modern scholars to admit that Jews attributed a body to their deity.[6]

The substance of the divine figure, the pieces from which it is constructed, are letter-pairs,[7] which embody, ironically, "the expression of all

5. See Dornsieff 1922:129 n. 2, where this practice is called writing (πληρωματικῶς), which he compares to the Hebrew terms "במילוי" or "מפורש." This exegetical method is found in later Jewish texts. See Jerome *Letter to Marcellus* for the divine name written Υοδηαυωαωηαυ.

6. See Graetz's comment cited in Chapter 5 note 45. For a recent discussion of this topic, see Wolfson 1994:13–51.

7. The twelve letter-pairs are similar to the letter-pairs used as the twelve zodiac signs, a point made by Franz Boll (1903:471).

that is unspeakable." These giant letters literally bridge the gap between the heavenly realm and the human realm.[8] The body stretches across the cosmos, linking the upper and lower worlds. Descriptions of giant divine figures abound in Late Antique texts, with everyone from Moses to Zeus appearing with bodies that fill up the entire cosmos.[9] Sometimes the figure appears to be the deity, other times an angel.[10] The ambiguity may be on purpose—that is, one way of dealing with queasiness in assigning a body to a deity is to shift the body language from the deity to an angelic figure or leave the text so ambiguous that it is difficult to tell exactly which figure is being discussed.

As in Origen and the rabbinic texts, this text refers to numerous different divine names, some more secret than others. The giant letter-body speaks a name that, unlike the hidden name, "we do know and speak." The highest-level name, as we learn later in the text, is beyond human comprehension and cannot be uttered by humans (*Against the Heresies* 1.15.1). The name that can be uttered is "Jesus Christ."

Marcus' fifth model divides the alphabet into three types of letters based on formal characteristics of pronunciation: mute, semi-vowels, and vowels. Each group of letters is the image of one of the three "powers that contain the entire numbers of the elements above" (1.14.5). The mute vowels, for instance, represent Pater (father) and Aletheia (truth) "because they are without voice, that is, of such a nature as cannot be uttered or pronounced" (1.14.5).[11] Language can have formal resemblances with cosmic powers even when both the sign and the object it stands for are unutterable. Language is iconic even at the unpronounced level of sounds.

Introducing still another model, the sixth, for cosmic letter-sounds, Marcus states that the heavens utter the sounds of the vowels.[12] Many ancient writers aligned the seven planets and the vowels, though the specific

8. Similarly, the letters from which the manifest world was formed are said to be infinite (Irenaeus *Against the Heresies* 1.14.2).

9. See Nilsson 1963 and Ezekiel the Tragedian.

10. See, for example, the description of Sandalphon (Scholem 1991:24 and M. Smith 1963:151). Alcibiades mentions a ninety-six-mile-high angel, complete with dimensions, who reveals a book to Elchasai (Luttikhuizen 1985 and Baumgarten 1986).

11. Subdivisions of letters into groups also appears in the *Book of Creation*, discussed below.

12. See Dornseiff 1922:82–83 and Blau 1914:130.

schemes were not identical.[13] According to Marcus, "The first heaven pronounced Alpha, the next to this Epsilon," and so on (*Against the Heresies* 1.14.7). When the cosmos speaks, it utters identifiable sounds but not semantically meaningful words. Humans can then make use of these sounds, as the soul calls out the letter Omega in order to get help from the upper world (1.14.8).

The name "Jesus" also has a numerical value based on the system known in Hebrew as *gematria,* where each letter has a numerical value; this is Marcus' seventh model. The derivation of the term *gematria* is unclear.[14] This numerical system for letters was originally Greek, based on the Greeks' standard use of letters to signify numbers. The practice was no doubt older than the coining of the term. According to Dornseiff, the oldest Greek example is found in eighth-century B.C.E. Miletus, and among Jews, the coin of the high priest Simon, 138–135 B.C.E. (1922:91–118).[15] According to Tertullian, Marcus claimed that Jesus said he was the Alpha and the Omega in order to introduce this system of exegesis (*Against the Heretics PL* 70A). Elsewhere Irenaeus reports that the Orphites and Sethites classify divine names by numerical value, with names that add up to less than 100 being "material" and hence of lesser value. *Gematria* is yet another nonsemantic use of language, and one that distinctly points to letters as the significant unit. Generating the numerical value of letters and words opens up endless interpretive possibilities and adds new levels of meaning to the text.

Some Jews, some Christians, and some Greco-Roman writers considered the method of *gematria* scientific. Artemidorus used the system for investigating dreams, for example (*Interpretation of Dreams* 2.70).[16] While *gematria* flourished all the way from medical to philosophical uses,[17] it was adopted with particular enthusiasm in rabbinic circles.[18]

13. Godwin (1991) attempts to find a standard schema based on the partial agreement between Marcus and Porphyry (Saturn/omega, Jupiter/upsilon, Mars/omicron, Sun/iota), but even these two writers do not entirely agree. For the identity of this Porphyry, who wrote a commentary on Dionysius of Thrace and is not the same as the famous Neoplatonist, see Bidez 1964 (1913), appendix, p. 72. See the comparative chart of Plutarch, Porphyry, and Lydus made by Ruelle 1889:42.

14. For some speculations, see Levias 1905.

15. See also Stambursky 1976.

16. See Gersh 1978:300.

17. For the use of *gematria* in medicine, see Censorinus *Concerning the Day of Birth* 7 and 14.

Not everyone accepted this mode of analysis, and attacking *gematria* was a way of ridiculing enemies. For example, Hippolytus, in his *Refutation of All Heresies,* cast scorn on this popular method as a means of castigating his opponents. He used the examples of computing the value of the names Agamemnon and Hector, presumably avoiding Christian examples so as not to confuse his rhetorical stance (4.14). The entire theology of Egyptian religion is based on a theory of numbers (4.43–44), and the Egyptians even calculated the numerical value of the word "deity." Hippolytus, galled by the notion that these computations were used to make predictions, summarized: "I think that there has been clearly expounded the mind of arithmeticians, who, by means of numbers and of names, suppose that they interpret life" (4.15). According to Hippolytus, using numbers and names to make predictions is as silly as looking at people's foreheads, a practice he also denounces but that had its supporters.[19]

While Theodorus found *gematria* valuable for investigating, for example, the meaning of the word "soul," his fellow Neoplatonist Iamblichus denounced it (*On the Timaeus,* frag. 57.9–22).[20] Iamblichus could easily point to the large number of words with the same numerical value but lacking any other connection. He did claim that Pythagoras taught a form of divination through numbers and that it was a great improvement over animal sacrifice as a means of divination (*On the Pythgorean Life* 54.21–25). How exactly this divination system worked is not stated. Theodorus' system was too contrived for Iamblichus, though theoretically numbers were divine.

Finally, for Marcus, the beginning of the story points to the end; when the sounds are reunited, a linguistic reunification that mirrors the cosmic reunification will be achieved. So too a rabbinic text claims that in the world to come everyone will pronounce the divine name (bPesachim 50a).

By the time Irenaeus has finished his summary of Marcus' ideas, entire sets of exegetical systems have been paraded in at least seven different models, each one of which can endlessly find cosmic meanings in a word

---

18. For Talmudic references, see bSuccah 28a, bSuccah 52b, and bShabbat 7a. See Levias 1905, Lieberman 1962:69–74, and Scholem 1972b.

19. Including, it should be noted, Pythagoreans and rabbis.

20. See the discussion by Shaw 1995:206–8.

or letter. These hidden, nonsemantically encoded meanings are the most important dimension of the holy text because they, and not the simple meanings of the words, represent divinity. Each image carries its "message" in its very structure. This does not mean that semantics does not play a part; it does, as soon as the system reaches the level of words.

Most significant for us is that all sorts of nonsemantic sounds and words now have a special connection to divinity and thus instantiate it on earth. These units can all be used in ritual to put divine power into play, pointing to a system of ritual language that relies not on first-person verbs, for example, but on the creative words and sounds that already were used in establishing the world itself.

The Jewish sources Marcus used are not preserved per se. We do have one extant text that intersects very closely with his ideas and expands them in a slightly different direction (toward divine names). The Hebrew text, *The Measurement of the [Divine] Dimension (Shi'ur Komah)*,[21] closely parallels Marcus' description of the Body of Truth. This time it is a male body with names for each limb, instead of a female body with letter-pairs.[22] In general outline the texts contain a limb-by-limb description of the deity, with the astronomical size of each limb ("the height of his neck is 130,000,000 parasangs") and the limb's name. The textual tradition of *Shi'ur Komah* is immensely complex with extensive editing; Marcus' discussion demonstrates that Jews developed this material long before the textual tradition was solidified.[23] The phrase *shi'ur komah* ap-

21. Translations of *Shi'ur Komah* are cited according to Cohen's edition (1985), including the specific text and line. Some of the translations have been adapted slightly. For a general introduction, see Scholem 1991:15–55.

22. Scholem, following Gaster 1971, cited Marcus' system as a parallel to *Shi'ur Komah* (Scholem 1954:65 and 1965b:37–39). Cohen (1983:23–25) rejects this comparison because of the difference between letter-pairs and name, a difference that the text itself mitigates. See Morray-Jones, forthcoming.

23. Scholem believed that this text was "the oldest possession of Jewish Gnosticism" (1954:66) and argued that the original version of the text was the version found in *Merkabah Rabba* (Scholem 1965a:6 and 1965b:27). Cohen has subsequently argued that the original text was composed in the early Gaonic period in Babylonia; it is best represented by British Museum manuscript 10675, which he dated to the tenth century (1985:5). Schäfer examined the manuscript and believes that it is probably from a much later date; he rejects the idea of a single original text (1988b:75–83). For an extensive critique of Cohen's reconstruction of the text history, see Herrmann (1988), who depends closely on Schäfer's assumptions (1988a). For another view, see the attempt to reconstruct some of the history of the editing process in Morray-Jones (forthcoming).

pears to refer to a *category* of knowledge (size/names of divine limbs) as much as to a specific text.[24] As if to clarify this confusion, all five textual versions used in Martin Cohen's recent edition use the device of question and answer. One states, for example, "I asked, teach me the measurement of our Creator . . . he said to me the *shi'ur komah*." Most important for our discussion, the variations among the textual versions show that the pragmatic implications of these texts are expressible in manifold specific wordings.[25]

The text as we have it includes two distinct levels of editing, each with its own pragmatic implications. At the first level, the text implicitly asks the question "What is divinity?" and answers it by presenting a divine language, by now familiar to us, of names and numbers. The names are individual icons of the limbs and, when they are arranged in order in the text, an icon of the overall body as well. The litany of limb names instantiates an entire language of creative words; each name embodies the pragmatic force of that particular "part" of the deity. God is conceived of as a collection of powerful forces (limbs), each force being captured in the name of the limb. Thus, the reciting of the list of names is a series of mini-transformational moments that "construct" the divine body "here" for viewing.[26] At each step they highlight the similarities between the divine body and the human body.[27]

24. Idel argues that the term is used generally for a secret dimension of Torah, mentioning yet another variant in the *Alphabet of R. Akiba*, "the measurement of the dimensions of the names of God" (1981:38). This material appears in texts with similar but distinct titles such as the *Book of the [Divine] Dimension (Sefer Ha-Komah)* and the *Book of the Measurement (Sefer Hashi'ur)*, and in the hekhalot (palace) texts, discussed at greater length in Chapter 5. Three of the five versions used by Cohen are part of hekhalot texts.

25. R. Ishmael said to him, "How much is the measurement of the body of the Holy One which is hidden from all men?" (*Sefer Raziel* 98–99); "This is the size of the [divine] body as stated in the Book of the Dimension" (*Sefer Hashi'ur* 1); R. Ishmael says, "Whosoever knows this measurement of his Creator and the glory of the Holy One?" (*Sefer Ha-qomah* 120–21); "And I said to him: 'Teach me the dimensions of the Holy One'" (*Siddur Rabba* 55–56); "I said to the Prince of the Torah, 'Rabbi, teach me the measurement of our creator,' and he said to me, 'the *shi'ur komah*'" (*Merkabah Rabba* 4–5).

26. See Morray-Jones 1992 and forthcoming.

27. In 3 Enoch 9–13 and 2 Enoch 2 we find similar "cosmicizing" of a human body. In 3 Enoch, Enoch-Metatron narrates that he was taken up from earth by the deity. The deity bestowed wisdom on him and then "laid his hand on me and blessed me with 1,365,000 blessings. I was enlarged and increased in size until I matched the world in length and breadth" (9:1–2; Alexander ed.). Enoch receives a new name, which contains the divine name, "The Lesser YH" ("My name is in him") (9:12), and a crown inscribed with the words "by which

At the second level, frames (added introductory comments) correlate knowledge of the text with specific goals. This correlation led Joseph Dan to characterize the text as "redeeming knowledge that assures its possessor happiness in this world and a share in the next—the world of redemption" (1979:72).[28] These frames seek to capture the perceived power of the names and to direct that power to a variety of goals. This mode of supplementation through framing is common; several of the texts examined below include later frames that redirect the pragmatic implications of a text.[29] Sometimes the frames add new goals that appear more mundane than the original goals. In this case Marcus might feel that the new frames somewhat degraded his revelation, because the revelation that was given to him alone is now being adapted for more everyday concerns. Such is the fate of many texts when the pragmatic implications are "recycled" for new purposes.

The most important extant Jewish text about the pragmatic implications of letters is the *Book of Creation*.[30] This short and almost completely cryptic text is so difficult to decipher and offers so many interpretations that analysis seems pure conjecture. Translations vary widely because it is hard to construe the Hebrew terminology and phrasing. Of significance to us in this discussion is not so much the interpretation of the details of the text as articulating its overall strategy. In short, the text investigates the Hebrew letters as the building blocks of creation. If we understand its strategy better we may understand why the text is so difficult to understand.

The subject of the *Book of Creation* is the creation of the world by the de-

---

heaven and earth were created" (13:1). Fossum (1985:245), following Scholem, notes the parallel passage in chapter 41 where the same letters are engraved on the throne of glory. In this text, the deity transforms Enoch by blessing him with a cosmic-size number of blessings. The transformation is marked by the bestowal of a divine name and the literal wearing of the effective letters. Reciting those letters permits a human to use the same transformational language as the deity.

28. See Cohen 1983:68–71, 167–85.

29. See the added frames in the *Mithras Liturgy*, discussed in Chapter 5.

30. For the dating debate, see, among others, Scholem 1954:75 and Pines 1989. Gruenwald (1971) published a critical edition, though others would reject his endeavor. For discussion of textual problems and attempts to create a stable text, see Gruenwald 1971 and 1973b and Sed 1973. Pines' thoughtful discussion points to Late Antique parallels for a dating of the basic ideas, and to a series of subsequent redactions after the sixth/seventh century (1989).

ity using a combination of what appears to be letters and numbers. Creation is described generating letter pairs from the divine name, which includes in it all letters and sounds. Some of these are familiar themes, but the text is so condensed that it demands interpretation in order to make any sense at all.

The building blocks of creation are described using the common Hebrew root "ספר, count/number." The text states: "He created His World in three books:[31] ספר (writings?) ספר (numbers?), ספר (speech?)." A new term is coined from this root *sefirah* (plural: *sefirot*), the implications of which are obscure. The ten *sefirot* appear to be a combination of the four elements (spirit, air, water, fire) with the six dimensions.

Scholars have struggled with exactly how best to translate the obscure *sefirot* and the various terms that play with the root "count/number." Translations of the former vary from "forms of expression" to "book."[32] The import of these phrases is that these creative elements are all related but distinguishable. This is itself a model of creation, where the same letters (root) can be used to build the various dimensions ("meanings") of the created world. When the ten *sefirot* are combined with the twenty-two letters of the alphabet, the result is the "thirty-two secrets paths of wisdom" by which the world was created. The text also includes one explicit reference to the creative power of the name, a theme now familiar to us: "and that is why everything which is created and everything which is spoken proceeds from one Name" (2.5).

The basic process described in the text is the movement from letter to natural element. The text explains how each letter instantiates a cosmic element. "M" represents water, "S" fire, and "A" air. Again, these are not symbolic modes of representation; the letters include in themselves the form and the sound of what they represent. These letters are identified as the "mother" letters, differentiated from the seven double letters and twelve simple letters.[33] The division of letters into subgroups is familiar from Marcus. Here the emphasis is on the elemental aspects of the letters.

31. Left untranslated, following Pines 1989.

32. Pines opted for the translation "book," although in this study he draws parallels with the Greek term ἔκστασις/extension (1989:81). Dornseiff related it to the Greek word for "sphere" (1922).

33. Another part of the text divides the letters into five groups based on the part of the mouth used to produce the sounds. This section may be a later addition to the text.

Creation can be brought about via letters because the letters are cosmic elements, and cosmic elements are letters.

A useful way of approaching the text is to view it as a dictionary of letters—that is, a dictionary in which the entries are letters and not words. Such a text presents immense challenges of translation and interpretation. The text must define the entries, the twenty-two letters of the alphabet and the ten *sefirot,* and then explain them.

To make the task even more complicated, the dictionary is not about semantics, which is the usual role of a dictionary. Letters have no semantic meanings. Instead, each entry tries to explain the creative (or pragmatic) implications of each letter. The entire text is therefore metapragmatic, delineating for the reader the basis by which letters can be used as pragmatic forces. It offers details as to how letters become manifest multidimensionally and ultimately "congeal" into the basic cosmic elements such as water and fire.

In general, the text is much denser than the already dense rendering of Marcus' system, because it attempts to give us a conception of language that is quite distinct from our own. It outlines the basis of a process that is not easily put into words. It is as if Marcus wrote a manual to answer the many questions his summary raises. For example, how specifically do the creative letters mediate between the unspoken divine world and the spoken material world? How does invisible speech transform into the visible world?

The text borders on incoherence because the processes it describes are beyond coherence. The best the text can do is hint at the creative processes. It presses beyond standard notions of semantic meaning, setting up analogies between the forms of language and the forms of natural elements. A dictionary that explicates the nonsemantic meanings of creative speech can do no more or less.

Before turning to comparative Greco-Roman examples, it is worth noting that the text intersects with two famous rabbinic anecdotes, both of which are tantalizing evidence of rabbinic speculation about the creative function of letters. The first states that Bezalel made the Tabernacle by combining letters (bBerakot 55a).[34] The brief comment gives only a bare-

---

34. The saying is assigned "Rav Judah said in the name of Rav," a third-century figure. The saying is followed by a short meditation on "wisdom" and "knowledge" being used in

bones description of the technique used by Bezalel. The story reveals little about the questions we are interested in (how did he use the letters? what exactly did they do?). We do learn that the making of the Tabernacle parallels the creation of the universe, which was also done via letters.

The second rabbinic anecdote refers to a work called "The Book of Creation": "On the eve of every Sabbath Rab Hanina and Rab Hoshaiah used to study the *Book of Creation* and created a three-year-old calf and ate it" (bSanhedrin 65a). It is extremely unlikely that their manual was the same as the extant work by that name, but the story does point to rabbinic figures who dabble in a written cosmogonic text. This story, along with several other anecdotes, holds out the possibility that rabbis can do the same creative work as the deity.[35]

Returning to the Neoplatonists, Theodorus of Arsine, a disciple of Iamblichus, found multiple meanings for a word based on analysis of the letters.[36] All his theories establish in different ways the iconic status of letters. Theodorus outlines for us in a systematic manner the meanings of letters, and their formal resemblance to cosmic reality. His ideas are preserved for us by Proclus, who scrutinized Theodorus' ideas at some length because their common mentor, Iamblichus, had criticized them.[37]

Theodorus argued for reasoning about the soul, from "letters, characters and numbers,"[38] a phrase reminiscent of the *Book of Creation*. He articulates the meaning of the word "soul" using three main approaches: the phonetic, the graphic, and the arithmetical.[39] According to a phonetic analysis, even the "rough breath" that begins the word "one" can be filled with meaning. It is an exact image of that which cannot be spoken, the supreme principle (*Commentary on the Timaeus* 2.274.16–23).[40] Just as in

---

creation (Exod 35:31 and Prov 3:19). Scholem argued that the letters were understood to come from the divine name, though that is not explicit in the anecdote (1972a:7).

35. This theme is discussed further in the Concluding Note.

36. For an introduction to Theodorus, see Praechter 1934.

37. Proclus *Commentary on the Timaeus* 2.274.10–278.25. On this, see Gersh 1978, excursus, pp. 289–304.

38. I follow here Gersh's suggestion for translation (1978:289 n. 2) contra Festugière 1967:318 n. 2.

39. Gersh dismisses as less important a fourth mode of analysis, noted by Festugière, which is based on the position of a letter in a word (1978:290 n. 5).

40. See Hadot 1968:97. Plotinus also mentions the "rough breath" at the beginning of the word "One," seeming to imply that it is commonly held to have this special meaning

Marcus' revelation, the linguistic representation of "a nature as cannot be uttered or pronounced" must itself be something that cannot be uttered. The linguistic unit, in this case the rough breathing, mirrors remote reality. The highest reality cannot be spoken, and neither can the rough breathing.

Theodorus' second mode of analysis is the graphic mode. Graphic analysis reveals that the circular motion of the soul is represented by the shape of the lines of y, which is spherical (*Commentary on the Timaeus* 2.276.2). Similarly, Theodosius Alexandrinus states that "A" is the "origin of multiplicity" because of its two diverging lines (Gersh 1978:277). Two additional examples are (1) the gematria of "E" is half of theta because E is half of its shape and (2) E's shape symbolizes the beam Pythagoreans are told not to step over (*Theologic Arithmetic* 40.9). The X is described in Proclus' *On the Republic* as the shape that occurs when the Demiurge divides the psychic material and then crosses it to form the "world soul" (*Commentary on the Republic* 2.143.20–24).[41] In the *Book of Creation*, the shape of the letter was significant, and here too the key to the creative process by which the demiurge made the world is encoded in letters.

The third type of meaning found in letters, according to Theodorus, is arithmetical, familiar from the examples of *gematria*. Theodorus' particular usage reduces a letter to its bases (subnumbers), generating new letters for analysis. Manipulating the numerical value of letters is one of the easiest modes of finding meaning in letters, given the common use in both Greek and Hebrew of letters for numbers. It is no coincidence that this method of analysis was much more widely accepted than Theodorus' other modes of analysis.

Iamblichus' criticism of Theodorus, as presented by Proclus, rejects some of the connections between letters and reality that Theodorus presumed to be meaningful. For Iamblichus, the connections are based on social convention;[42] only those that are "natural" (iconic) can tell us something about reality. For example, Iamblichus argued, as noted above,

---

(*Enneads* 5.8.4, 6). He also mentions the special representational status of Egyptian hieroglyphs (*agalmata*). He himself, however, favored the mind's intuition as a mode of apprehending the One (5.5.5.19–27). See Hirschle 1979:39–42 and Ferwerda 1982:57.

41. See Gersh 1978:297.

42. In the Peircean terms of this study, signs that represent based on social convention are called symbols.

words could have the same number of letters without this having any significance. The shapes of letters change over time, showing that they are based on social convention. To label someone else's icons as mere conventional symbols, as in Iamblichus' attack, is to sever Theodorus' claims about a connection to reality. In Peircean terms, the signs Theodorus considers to be icons are merely conventional symbols for Iamblichus and therefore cannot represent the highest levels of reality.

As always, linguistic theories will have ritual implications. Iamblichus rejects certain ritual uses of language, such as the idea of standing on characters while reciting words (*On the Mysteries* 3.13; 129.14–132.2) Proclus categorically states: "It is unsafe to argue dialectically from characters" (*Commentary on the Timaeus* 2.278.9). The characters do not have any formal resemblance to any level of reality, so they cannot have any special function.

Iamblichus preserves his own iconic notions of language and embraces some connections between language and reality. It is not surprising that central among them are names. Even when they do not appear to make sense to humans, they are not without sense to gods (*On the Mysteries* 7.4.254.17–255.6). Here Iamblichus joins Origen and the many other thinkers who posit that it is not the semantic content of names that gives them significance, but instead their power to manifest divinity on earth.[43] The key for Iamblichus is that names are able to do this because they are "natural" representations of the deity and not based on convention.

Nicomachus, whose early use of the word "theurgy" was discussed above, also justifies the use of vowel sounds in rituals.

And the tones of the seven spheres, each of which by nature produces a particular sound, are the sources of the nomenclature of the vowels. These are described as unpronounceable in themselves and in all their combinations by wise men since the tone in this context performs a role analogous to that of the monad in number, the point in geometry and the letter in grammar. However, when they are combined with the materiality of the consonants just as soul is combined with body and harmony with strings—the one producing a creature,

43. See Shaw 1995:110, 179.

the other notes and melodies—they have potencies which are efficacious and perfective of divine things. Thus whenever the theurgists
are conducting such acts of worship they make invocation symbolically with hissing, clucking, and inarticulate and discordant sounds.[44]

Language is a metaphor for the state of the cosmos as both material and
immaterial at the same time. The effective dimension is that which more
closely resembles the soul and not the body.

The Hebrew name theory and the Greek vowel theory merge when the
Hebrew divine name is thought to consist of only vowels. A specific nexus
between the four-letter Jewish divine name and the seven Greek vowels
appears, for example, in Eusebius' statement that the Jewish divine name
consists of seven vowels reduced to four (*Preparation for the Gospels*
11.6). As both vowels and sounds of the divine names, these four letters
are doubly effective. A more general theory of the efficacy of vowels is
found in Philo, who simply stated that vowels are the best and most effective letters (*Allegorical Interpretation* 1.14).[45]

All the theories outlined here are put to work in various Late Antique
ritual texts where vowels are employed. The use of vowel sounds in rituals was widespread enough that we find diverse kinds of evidence for it.
Demetrius of Phalerium believed that the pleasing use of vowels in rituals
came from Egypt, reversing the common trope that bad ritual practices
(magic) comes from Egypt: "In Egypt the priests, when singing hymns in
praise of the gods, employ the seven vowels, which they utter in due suc-
cession; and the sound of these letters is so euphonius that men listen to it
in place of flute and lyre" (*On Style* 71).

A Jewish-influenced prayer from the Greek papyri (mid-third to mid-
fourth century) connects hidden divine names, vowels, and cosmic forces
(*PGM* 13.760–932).[46] The basic thrust of the prayer is identification with

44. *Greek Writers on Music* 276.8–18. Jan; translation from Gersh (1978:295). See
Dornseiff 1922:52.
45. Philo may also have written a treatise, now lost, on the meaning of letters (Wutz
1914).
46. See the next chapter for more uses of vowels in rituals. Secret vowel-based divine
names also appear in several of the Nag Hammadi texts, including the *Gospel of the Egyptians* (3.2.43–44, 66) and *Discourse on the Eighth and Ninth* (6.6.61; 60.17–61.17).

a divinity by the reciter who knows the secret name. The prayer is entitled "Here is the instruction [for recitation] of the heptagram," a term that appears to refer to the seven vowels. The prayer begins with a reference to the name being "hidden and unspeakable" for humans (764–65). Midway in the text, it invokes the divine name of vowels: "Yours is the eternal processional way in which your seven-lettered name is established for the harmony of the seven sounds [of the planets that utter] their voices according to the 28 forms of the moon SAR APHARA APHARA" (*PGM* 775–80).[47]

Further on in the prayer the secret name reappears as "a unique phylactery in my heart," which guarantees identification of the reciter and the divinity (you are I, and I am you) (795–96). The name also resides in the reciter's soul (800). In the closing, the reciter claims to have "the power of Abraham, Isaac and Jacob" and "the great god demon Iao."[48] This prayer asks for quite an array of blessings, including "health no magic can harm, well-being, prosperity, glory, victory, power, sex appeal" (804).

Repeatedly we have seen that letters and their sounds are significant because they have more than simple, worldly (semantic) meaning. Instead, cosmic sounds are important because they are in fact cosmic. They represent the divine world on earth, being icons of some aspects of that world. Sounds can "do things" because they are icons of divinity, audible and accessible bits of the inaudible and inaccessible divine world. Though distinctions between words and letters are confused, language does not have to be destroyed in order to find reality. Instead, language *is* reality, and particularly at the level of an individual letter and its sounds. The basic structure of the cosmos is contained in, and not distorted by, the basic element of language: sound.

47. The translation cited here is by Morton Smith (Betz 1986:190). Gersh also mentions this phrase in his discussion of phonetic analysis below (1978:294). See Dornseiff 1922:37.

48. On the popularity of the divine name Iao, see M. Smith 1973:233. See Dieterich 1891:68–71 on *PGM* 5:460–85. According to Pistis Sophia 136, Jesus spoke the name "Iao" to the four directions.

5
USING NAMES, LETTERS, AND PRAISE:
THE LANGUAGE OF ASCENT

Tell the mystery, and seal yourself
with this seal, this is his name
—The Second Book of Jeu 52 (GCS 13.315–21)

T he heavenly ascent by Rabbi Nehunya in *Hekhalot Rabbati* has become something of a classic, first championed by Gershom Scholem and since then the subject of much discussion.[1] This text is part of the loosely defined collection of Hebrew texts referred to as *hekhalot* (palace) texts or *merkabah* (chariot) texts, which describe the heavenly realm, the liturgy of the heavenly chorus, rites for calling down the angelic figure the Prince of the Torah, and assorted other esoteric traditions.[2] In Rabbi Nehunya's ascent,[3] he separates his body from his soul and traverses the fiery and terrifying heavens, describing them as he goes.[4] In another ascent text, the *Mithras Liturgy*, we witness the bodily transformation during ascent of a human to heaven, who then becomes a heavenly being. Employing special language functions is the heart of the efficacy of both these ascents, including such now-familiar techniques as reciting divine names and letter-sounds. The rituals depend on an additional mode of divine language: descriptions of the angelic cult in heaven and its liturgy, found already in the Dead Sea Scrolls. Harnessing divine language permits the human practitioners to transcend their earthly existence and become part of the heavenly world.

1. See especially Scholem 1954 and M. Smith 1963. See also the studies cited below.
2. For summaries, see Schäfer 1992, and on the angelology, see Elior 1994.
3. The Hebrew term used is "descent." For Scholem's speculations on this term, which have not been superseded, see 1954:46–47 and 1965a:20 n. 1.
4. James Tabor outlines the basic pattern of Late Antique ascent (1986:87).

Ascent to the heavens was a common postbiblical literary theme reflecting the elaborate systems of heavens that emerged after the third century B.C.E.[5] Revelatory texts attributed to biblical characters were often cast as ascents.[6] Characteristically the enigmatic phrase "Enoch walked with God" (Gen 5:24) was expanded in later texts to a lengthy and detailed presentation of what Enoch saw and learned on an extended tour of the cosmos.[7]

Jewish descriptions of ascent were by no means unique; numerous Greco-Roman and Christian texts were structured as trips taken by individuals to the upper realms.[8] The formats of these ascents varied widely. Heroic figures were portrayed as being snatched up into the heavens, usually in the distant past. Some ascents happened during the character's life, some after death;[9] the setting could be a dream, a vision, or even part of a philosophical investigation.[10]

Although its origins are somewhat murky, ascent emerged as a ritual practice by the first century C.E., when it was no longer something attributed only to figures from the distant past. Exactly how, or when, the ritual practice of ascent emerged is not clear. The complex relationship between the literary themes of ascent and the development of rituals is perforce shrouded in mystery because so few texts survive.[11] Ascent was no longer conceived of as something that happened only to past heroes. In the Dead Sea Scrolls we see claims that humans can see the heavenly world, making ascent a goal that could be actively sought out and affected by human action.[12] New types of evidence about ascent emerge by the first century C.E., including first-person claims of ascents by historical

5. See Nilsson 1948:96–110 for a summary of the Greek version of this cosmology; for Jewish versions, see the many descriptions of the multiple heavens in the pseudepigraphical texts and rabbinic texts.

6. See Segal 1980 for a review of texts that include ascents.

7. See 1 Enoch in Charlesworth 1985, as well as the other Enoch texts.

8. For additional Greco-Roman references to ascent, see Johnston 1997:116 n. 4, and for ascent as a theme in earlier Greek texts, see ibid., 176 n. 35.

9. For ascent after death attributed to the "Orphians," see *Against Celsus* 6.24–38.

10. See M. Smith 1981.

11. The Qumran texts give us a hint as to how much of ritual and liturgy is lost to us.

12. Human volition does not negate the need for divine permission and even help in the highest realm.

figures,[13] liturgical texts structured as ascents,[14] and deification-by-ascent rituals.[15]

The possible reasons for and meaning of the ascent rituals were diverse. In the multiheavened Late Antique cosmology, a trip to the heavenly realm was a way to gain access to the angelic court and its occupants. Ascent was sometimes envisioned as a means for a human either to return to his "home" or to achieve a new, heightened status by the trip.[16] Sometimes ascent was believed to happen only after a person died, and therefore the ritual would be enacted only after death. The divinization of the Roman emperors was a highly visible example of ascent as transformation after death.[17]

Ascent could be a goal in itself, as in the philosophical life,[18] or a process undertaken in the name of other goals, such as learning about the future.[19] Some Jews wanted to ascend because they, like other residents of the Greco-Roman world, wanted to have closer contact with the deity who resided in the seventh heaven.[20] Ascent could have been undertaken in order to gain immortality.[21] The widespread belief in astral immortality held out the possibility that someone could ascend into the heavens and become an immortal star (4 Macc 17:5). Undertaking an ascent while still alive could function as proof that someone was godlike. For Philo, ascent was a means of divinization (*Questions on Exodus* 40).

Literary scholars often have limited specific interest in issues of ritual ef-

13. See the claim of Paul in 2 Corinthians 12:2–4 and the discussion of this text as an ascent by Paul in Tabor 1986.

14. See the *Songs of the Sabbath Sacrifice,* discussed below.

15. On the deification rituals of the Roman Emperors, see Bickerman 1929 and more recently Price 1984 and 1987.

16. See J. Z. Smith 1974:749.

17. See the Roman senator's report that he saw Augustus ascending to the heavens (Suetonius *Augustus* 100.4 and Dio Cassius *History* 56.46.2).

18. For Apollonius of Tyana's ascent, see Philostratus *Life of Apollonius of Tyna* 8.30 (M. Smith 1981:409).

19. This is a theme in some of the texts discussed below.

20. Martha Himmelfarb opts for a philosophical, almost existential, meaning of ascent (1993). She turns to Goodenough's view of Philo, for whom ascent was a way to solve the problem of the perception of God's inaccessibility. Here she follows earlier scholars, such as J. Z. Smith and Morton Smith. This analysis is more convincing than elsewhere in her book, where she posits that the daily lives of Jews may have been unsatisfactory and that that may have led them to imagine themselves "like the glorious ones" (1993:114).

21. Among hekhalot texts, this particular claim is found most clearly in claims about the world to come.

ficacy. The result is that the explanations of ascent rituals are based on very narrow concepts of efficacy. The most common explanation of ascent rituals is that they work by means of a trance.[22] Certain procedures, usually deprivational, induce a trance during which an individual thinks he is traversing the heavens.[23] Trance is sometimes presented as the best rational explanation for seemingly irrational rituals (people become dizzy and think they are ascending). These explanations, like comparisons with shamanistic "trips" in oral cultures, tend to obscure the historically specific nature of rituals.[24] As appealing as this idea seems, there is little direct evidence of trance in the texts.[25]

Morton Smith astutely observed that when Rabbi Nehunya's companions want to ask him a question they must carefully interrupt him because he is not simply talking about an ascent but ascending while he talks (1963:145). How does his "talk" make him ascend? At first glance, this is not a promising clue about techniques. We find no complex instructions, such as having to go to a particular place, wear certain clothing, or bring some special objects.[26] However, the previous chapters have prepared us for ideas about the efficacy of words, which we now see here in action: ascent is achieved primarily based on the repetition of vowel sounds, divine names, and, in this case, heavenly liturgy.[27]

22. This explanation goes back as far as Bousset 1901.

23. Philip Alexander uses the notion of trance to explain how ascent works in 3 Enoch. He states: "Given the rigorous preparations for the ascent, the sense of anticipation and the aura of mystery and awe with which the act was surrounded, this repetition would have been potent enough to send the adepts into trance. Its efficacy would have been magnified if, as Hai Gaon asserts, the mystics recited the hymns with their heads between their knees, in the manner of Elijah on Mount Carmel, thus constricting their breathing" (1983b:233).

24. It seems impossible to me to distinguish between a "trance ascent," which appears be a pseudo-ascent, and an ecstatic rapture, where someone actually travels somewhere" (Schäfer 1992:154–55).

25. Support for the trance theory is found in later Jewish texts, such as Hai Gaon's tenth-century commentary (note 23 above). These later explanations of technique may represent reinterpretations of ascent developed when the earlier basis of efficacy was no longer understood or had simply changed.

26. *Ma'aseh Merkabah* has a single reference to fasting in an Aramaic section (19).

27. Some of Scholem's heirs have been eager to find evidence of ascent techniques in any text that mentions ascent. Martha Himmelfarb has cautioned against these arguments, pointing to the literary nature of many references to ascent (1993). Her caution is warranted in the case of those narrative texts where ascent is only a literary topos. A clear distinction should be kept in mind between a literary reference to a person ascending and a ritual text where ascent is structured into the text as a practice.

The technique of reciting words in order to ascend appears in the first extant ascent text, *Songs of the Sabbath Sacrifice* (4Q400–407).[28] The *Songs* are among the earliest extant Jewish liturgy and display some of the strategies Jews used in creating liturgy.[29] In fact, they are precious evidence because no public liturgy besides the Qumran scrolls is extant from the first centuries c.e.[30] The *Songs* is a liturgical collection of thirteen hymns containing intricate descriptions of the angelic cult in heaven. The hymns detail the seven priesthoods along with other participants in the heavenly cult, ending with a description of the heavenly temple (based on Ex 40–48). All the participants in the heavenly court are busily engaged in singing praises to God.

The image of a heavenly chorus goes back to the Hebrew Scriptures. The most famous and oft-repeated instance is Isaiah's report that the angels recite "Holy, holy, holy is the Lord of Hosts, the whole earth is full of his glory" (Isa 6:3). The image of a heavenly court, complete with liturgy and other cultic activities, was extensively developed in Jewish and Christian texts. The heavenly cult superseded the earthly cult, with angels offering their own versions of sacrifice complete with continual praise.[31] As we would expect based on all the descriptions of heavenly sounds examined in the previous chapters, the heavenly sounds were both much more extensive and much more cryptic than Isaiah's "Holy, holy, holy." For example, *Apocalypse of Abraham* 15:7 describes the sound of heaven as "a sound of words I knew not."[32]

28. This text was found in multiple copies. See the critical edition by Newsom 1985.

29. Newsom believes, despite the extreme ambiguity of the case, that the scales tip in favor of the document's not being a product of the sectarian community. The bases for this is that a copy was found at Masada, and the particular manner in which God's name is recorded (Newsom 1990b). It is a mistake to marginalize the text as more "sectarian" than other contemporary texts.

30. Talmon writes: "The absence of codification, definition and binding formulation may account for the fact that the text of not even one Jewish public prayer from before the destruction of the Second Temple, or for that matter from before the middle of the first millennium c.e., has been preserved" (1978:271). Some rabbinic circles may have actively repressed liturgy that they felt was not sufficiently under their control or did not represent their interests.

31. In addition to the Qumran descriptions, rabbinic descriptions of the angelic cult, complete with its sacrifice of souls, are collected in Aptowizer (1930–31).

32. For other descriptions of the heavenly chorus and its language, see Origen *Against Celsus* 7.9, Lucian *Alexander the False Prophet* 13, Philo *Who Is the Heir* 259–66, *Testament of Job* 48–50, and *Corpus Hermeticum* 1.26.

The *Songs* describe the cultic heavenly world in detail. Newsom concludes: "What characterizes the Sabbath Shirot is description—insistent and often vivid description of angelic praise and blessing, of the heavenly temple, its structures and appurtenances, the *merkabah,* the procession of the angels, the splendid vestments of the celestial high priests, and so forth" (1985:64). The seventh Song, for example, describes how the cherubim and ophanim, the mythical beasts who carry the deity's throne, and even the heavenly furniture praise the deity:

> And all the crafted furnishing of the debir [inner sanctum] hasten (to join) with wondrous psalms in the debi[r . . .] of wonder, debir to debir with the sound of holy multitudes. And all their craft furnishing. [. . .] And the chariots of His debir give praise together, and their cherubim and thei[r] ophanim bless wondrously [. . .] the chiefs of the divine structure. And they praise him in His holy debir. (*Songs of the Sabbath Sacrifice* 4Q403 1.2.13–15 [Newsom 1985:229])

Based on the preliminary publication of fragments of the text, Morton Smith claimed that the text was an ascent text (1981:412). The editor of the critical edition of the fragments, Newsom, came to a similar conclusion with a different nuance.[33] That the text is liturgy is widely accepted; that the liturgy was used as part of a ritual aimed at ascent is more controversial.[34] According to Newsom, the description of the celestial high priest is the climax of a step-by-step ascent. The ascent by the individual reciting the text culminates in a vision of the innermost heavenly temple and its cult. The language of the text creates "the experience of being present in the heavenly temple and in the presence of the angelic priests who serve there" (1990b:115).[35] Baumgarten (1988) similarly observes that the worshiper is transmitted progressively through the heavens by the text. How exactly can we account for what these scholars are claiming—that

33. See Newsom 1985:59–72 for a discussion of its liturgical use.

34. Schiffman (1982) and Himmelfarb (1993) reject the notion that ascent was a ritual practice in this text.

35. Newsom (1985:63–64) also discusses the shared priestly community of angels and humans.

is, what is the basis of the perceived efficacy of the *Songs* to transport their reciter into the heavenly world?

Both the structure and the language of the text contribute to the effect of seeing the upper realm, which, given the cosmology, necessitates an ascent. Surveying the *Songs* quickly gives one an impression of their structure: an exact image of the structure of the heavenly world, mapping out the increasingly holy and central level of the cult.[36] Patterns of seven layers structure the text:

> Praise [the God of elim,
> O you seven priesthood of his inner sanctum . . .] loftiness,
> seven wondrous territories according to the ordinances of His
> sanctuaries [the chiefs of the princes of the (wondrous)
> priesthoods] [. . .]
> seven priest[hoods] in the wondrous sanctuary for the seven
> holy councils. . . .
> And the tongue of the first [angelic prince] will grow strong
> sevenfold [joining] with the tongue of the one who is second
> to him.
> And the tongue of the one who is second with respect to him
> will grow strong sevenfold from [the sound of] the one who is
> third with respect to him.

> (*Songs of the Sabbath Sacrifice* 4Q403
> 1.2.20–28 [Newsom 1985: 230])

Such repetitive patterns are the heart of many ritual texts since they outline the "culturally derived aspects of the cosmologies" (Tambiah 1985:142). In this case the culturally derived aspect of the cosmology is the entire cosmology, because the "here" of the ritual takes place in the heavenly realm. The entire ritual "takes place" in a place that has been constructed by reference to the reciter's systematic mapping of it.[37]

---

36. This is also true of later ascent texts, as, for example, the layer after layer of flaming chariots depicted in *Ma'aseh Merkabah*.

37. The repetitious nature of the text is sometimes presumed to point toward trance, as noted above. The point being made here is that ritual texts are repetitious in part because that repetition provides the essential poetic structure for the ritual context.

The ascent is put into action by the act of reciting the liturgy. As Newsom states, the imperative verb forms at the start of each hymn activate that particular hymn (that is, "Praise . . ."), coordinating human activity and divine activity. Finishing the recitation is linked with having seen the most holy level of cult. The *Songs* are a special form of socially conceived action by which the context of the heavenly world, complete with the angelic chorus and cult, is invoked as a place where the reciter *has* been. Recitation of the hymns results in construction of the special (heavenly) context for human liturgy. The projection moves from the language of the ritual to the cosmos, modeling in the *Songs* not only every detail of the heavenly cosmos but also the interactions that take place within it.

At the same time, the *Songs* have the semblance of being free of any particular earthly context—that is, they do not seem to be tied to a specific time or space. Recitation of the *Songs* seems to take place suspended in time and abstracted from a clear historical setting. The earthly context in which the hymns are sung is set aside and not mentioned.[38] The very lack of any earthly dimension to the cosmology emphasizes the heavenly world, which is the only reality for the ritual.[39]

Priestly status seems to be a key to this ascent, because the reciters are the earthly parallels to the heavenly priests.[40] The priests who recite the text, presumably as a group,[41] overcome the horizontal divisions between earthly beings and heavenly beings enabling them, literally, to watch the heavenly cult unfold. Pointing out the superior status of the highest angels over the human priests preserves some humility.[42] However, the special human and angelic cohort is higher than both other humans and other heavenly groups because they are in the presence of the highest cult.

When the ascent practitioner is not a priest, the importance of angelic

38. See Newsom on avoiding explicit references to the human community (1990b:115).
39. Richard Parmentier explains: "In many cases the denial of referential specifically enables rituals to concentrate on reference to eternal or universal truths, in much the same way that, as Mukarovsky argued, the aesthetic function of a work of art is freed from particular denotational value" (1994:131).
40. Elior has written most extensively and persuasively on the importance of priestly themes in this literature (1999). Descriptions of heavenly liturgy do not necessitate an origin or use only in priestly circles, though in the *Songs* the priestly connection is clear.
41. Note the frequent use of the plural.
42. See the self-critical comment made by the priests in the second *Song*.

priests is, not surprisingly, diminished. A more general model of heavenly liturgy as angelic but not priestly praise will be exploited in later ascent texts.[43]

The purpose of the ascent in the *Songs* is never made explicit. To the extent that the cult was understood to take place in heaven, having intimate knowledge of that cult was a necessity for any priest on earth. The hymns also undoubtedly reinforce the authority of those who used them (Newsom 1990b). In another Qumran text (1QSb), blessings transform a person into a being like the "angel of the presence." It is difficult to imagine that being part of the angelic chorus, or being like the angel of presence, is anything less than a mark that the reciter of the hymns has become immortal. Yet another Qumran text (4Qm[a] *War Scroll variant*) describes an individual who becomes one of the "gods" (אלים) via an ascent (M. Smith 1990). The phrase "I shall be reckoned with gods and established in the holy congregation" (frag. 11, col. 1, 13–14) is a claim that, as Morton Smith points out, makes the most sense coming from someone originally mortal. This text is a report of a transformation of a human who is established in the heavenly cult, though we are not told exactly how this happened.

In all these examples, the Qumran texts present critical evidence about the use of "talk" to transform an earthly speaker. Sometimes such talk is explicit descriptions of the heavenly cult, other times it seems to be a more general use of blessings, which are another subcategory of heavenly liturgy. All this talk is not human talk, but instead the copying of the language of the upper realm.

Against the contours of the *Songs*, the strategies used in Rabbi Nehunya's ascent emerge as variations on the same themes of divine "talk." The rabbi's ascent appears in *Hekhalot Rabbati,* yet another Jewish text that presents foreboding challenges.[44] Like all the *hekhalot* texts, this one

---

43. In the *Book of Secrets*, chap. 6, no priestly motifs remain in the heavenly liturgy. In parallel rabbinic texts, the priestly themes remain (for these, see Elior 1990); new rabbinic criteria of association ultimately supplant them, though rabbis are always willing to lay claim to the priestly authority.

44. The Hebrew text is available in Schäfer 1981:81–280 and the German translation, Schäfer 1987–91, vol. 2. On its redaction, see Schäfer 1988a:63–74 and Gruenwald 1980:150–73. The text begins with a long series of hymns introduced as being appropriate

is difficult to date, difficult to translate, and exhibits particularly thorny
problems with regard to the manuscript traditions. None of the hekhalot
texts are extant from Late Antiquity; they must be reconstructed from
much later, mainly thirteenth- and fourteenth-century manuscripts
(Schäfer 1981). Given the controversy that surrounds these texts, it is necessary to pause and discuss the nature of the evidence before examining
Rabbi Nehunya's ascent.

Scholars continue to debate the viability of reconstructing Late Antique texts from late medieval manuscripts, a debate loaded with the
added burden that the material is viewed with a general suspicion. Gershom Scholem consistently pressed for not only a Late Antique but even
a pre-Christian date, to implicate a Jewish origin for the material (1954).
To bolster his argument and to make the exotic texts appear more main-
stream, whenever possible he cited parallels to the normative rabbinic
texts, such as the Mishnah and the Talmud (the earlier the rabbinic text,
the better).

Many of Scholem's points have become clichés, with widespread
agreement that Late Antique Jews engaged in practices and had beliefs
that were, pre-Scholem, denounced as nonsense or late medieval degeneration of Judaism. No one argues anymore that these texts were borrowed
from Islamic material, for example, nor would anyone describe them, as
Graetz did, with such terms as "childish," "degenerate," or "monstros-
ity."[45] However, not everyone is ready to accept Scholem's early dating of
the hekhalot texts (first through third centuries) or to place them at more
than the very fringes of Judaism.[46]

Rejection of Scholem's early dating of the material in the hekhalot
texts revolves around the status of the textual evidence. Peter Schäfer,

---

for ascent, and then shifts to a series of apocalypses that give "historical" settings for specific
ascents, such as the story that after the Romans had seized several scholars R. Ishmael was
then sent to descend and find out why God had permitted this to happen (par. 107, sec. 5).
The text returns to hymns again, *Shi'ur Komah* material, more hymns, descriptions of a
prayer ritual in heaven, and lists of divine names. Only then does the main ascent begin (par.
198, sec. 13). After the main ascent, the text concludes with some final hymns and two appended stories about enhancing memory.

45. Graetz on *Shi'ur Komah*, cited in Cohen 1983:vi.

46. See also the discussion of the marginalizing of selected texts in modern scholarship in
the Introduction.

for example, questions whether the texts ever existed in "original" editions, given the high number of variants found in the various manuscripts (1981). He abandoned the idea of a single original text and presents the text in synoptic form instead. This fluidity of tradition is seen as evidence that it is impossible to reconstruct Late Antique versions of the texts. Hence, it is unknown what, if anything, goes back to the first centuries.

Scholars have also attacked the connections Scholem attempted to draw between the hekhalot material and the more familiar rabbinic texts.[47] For example, David Halperin (1980) argued, based on redaction criticism, that the Mishnaic, Talmudic, and Midrashic references to hekhalot material appear in the later strata of the rabbinic texts and thus are not evidence of early rabbinic practice.[48] Thus the classic Talmudic story about four rabbis who went to Paradise was not originally a story of a heavenly ascent vision, as Scholem argued (1965a:14–19), but simply an allegory about the practice of biblical exegesis. Only in later interpretations was the story understood to refer to an ascent practice. Early rabbinic Judaism remains orthodox. In a similar vein, Schäfer posits a historical context of a fringe group of "mystics" versus "normative" rabbinic Jews, and this reconstruction determines the contours of all the themes he elaborates from the hekhalot material.[49]

Despite the claims that the methods of textual criticism hold out seemingly scientific proof of the development of traditions, the continuing debates prove that it is possible to come to more than one conclusion about the history of the texts. Recently, there has been resurgence in support for the position that the texts have sufficient coherence to be viewed as identifiable texts from the first centuries. Morray-Jones (1992, 1993) offers an alternative reconstruction of the editing of the rabbinic texts that is more

---

47. See Swartz 1996:214 for a brief comparison of purity issues in these texts and in other rabbinic texts.

48. See the review in Elior 1990 and the critique by Neusner 1985:172–95.

49. Schäfer's view (1991) that the person ascending rejects traditional means and tries instead to storm heaven depends upon an extremely narrow definition of traditional practices. He claims that it is accepted by all scholars that ascent moves between two poles: the pure form and the magical. Yet even Schäfer's pure form, ascent via the use of hymns, is "magical" by his own criteria. On his narrow view of traditional practices, see Lesses 1998:35–43.

favorable to Scholem's thesis.[50] Davila (1993) has recently argued for a critical edition of *Hekhalot Rabbati.*

Perhaps the textual controversy has been asked to bear too much weight.[51] Whether the reference to a "chariot" vision is late or early in a specific rabbinic text tells us only about the redaction of that particular text.[52] Jews engaged in extensive speculation about the heavenly chariot and palaces for centuries before it was recorded in rabbinic texts. Rachel Elior maintains that "an uninterrupted line can be drawn from the religious-literary activity of the last centuries B.C.E., associated directly and indirectly, with the merkabah tradition, to the mystical works of the first centuries C.E. known as hekhalot and merkavah literature" (1999:105).[53] Rabbinic texts begin to polemicize about ascent practices in the third century, but that does not mean the practices began then.[54] This does not make the esoteric material a late intrusion into a monolithic rabbinic Judaism. It does point to contemporary power struggles about religious rituals directed toward heavenly and earthly power. The editing and reshaping of ritual texts probably continued for centuries, driven by forces far removed from the earlier speculative traditions.

Morton Smith dates one of the apocalyptic sections of *Hekhalot Rabbati* to the mid-fourth century, but he also argued, following Scholem,

50. Morray-Jones has been critiqued in turn by Goshen-Gottstein 1995, who argues that the "paradise" story about Jewish mysticism appears only in the Talmudic version. See also Alexander's discussion of the relationship between 3 Enoch and Talmudic traditions (1987b).

51. See, for example, the statement by Goshen-Gottstein that "the answer to the question of how much mysticism existed in rabbinic Judaism depends on the interpretation of this story" (1995:69). Schäfer does not demonstrate that the hekhalot materials fall outside the spectrum of variants found in other manuscript traditions. In the case of other texts, considerations of "orthodoxy" spurred the creation of modern normative critical editions that obscured the vast number of variants. Perhaps the lesson from the hekhalot texts is that many other Late Antique texts would benefit from synoptic presentation.

52. In addition, rabbinic texts are not simple reflections of first-century practices, esoteric or otherwise. With the compilation of the Mishnah dated to the mid-third century, and its origins back in the previous two centuries obscure, rabbinic literature generally is dated "later" and thus, oddly enough, closer to the common dating of the hekhalot texts.

53. For a recent collection of the evidence, see Elior 1999. Whether all this literature was produced, as she claims, by secessionist priestly circles is open to debate. Speculation about the heavenly Temple probably occurred in many circles.

54. See Goshen-Gottstein 1995 and his careful argument that the Tosefta shows debates over the legitimacy of ascent practices.

that the other sections contained material going back to the first century (1963:148). References to similar techniques and ritual practices in, among others, Greco-Roman[55] and Christian writers[56] point to the middle of the third century as a possible time frame for composition of the ascent sections. By this time the strategy of the *Songs* had evolved considerably. The ascent is part of a composite text containing material that was originally written in Palestine and later expanded in Babylonia.[57] Much denser poetic constructions than the *Songs*, the hymns pile up words of praise so intricately that they are difficult to parse and translate.

> King adorned, clothed in royal tribute,
> Honored with the embroidery of song,
> Wreathed with majesty and honor,
> A wreath of sublimity and a crown of awesomeness.
> Because his name is pleasing to him,
> and his remembrance is sweet to him,
> And his throne is adornment to him,
> and his [palace] is honor to him,
> And his glory is desirous to him,
> and his magnificence is becoming to him,
> and his strength is pleasing to him,
> and his servants sweetly sing to him.

(par. 252)

Scholem's heirs have attempted to refine his rudimentary structural analysis by either further explicating the theme of heavenly praise[58] or detailing

---

55. Parallels with the *Mithras Liturgy* are cited below.

56. Use of the names of the gatekeepers to travel around the heavens is mentioned by Origen. Arnobius of Sicca *Against the Nations* 2.62 mentions the use of hymns in ascent.

57. Note the references to "the mangers of Caesarea" and "the gates of Caesarea" (par. 214). Alexander believes that the story in sections 5–6 is also of Palestinian origin (1983b:222).

58. Grozinger expands Scholem's point, outlining the centrality of images of song in the hymns (1987).

the structures of the hymns.[59] The latter task is particularly difficult because there are many possible ways of arranging the short praise-phrases
and noun-pairs found throughout the hymns.[60] The praise-phrases and
noun-pairs can be built up into seemingly endless kinds of larger structures based on the inclination of the editor. Some editors particularly liked
names and extended the name sections.

If it was possible to ascend with the *Songs,* what does the later ascent
liturgy show in terms of new strategies and notions of efficacious language? The *Songs* consist of descriptions of the heavenly cult but include
no direct citations of angelic praise.[61] In contrast, the hekhalot hymns are
repetitions of the exact words of the heavenly liturgy. Scholars often miss
the sheer cleverness of this strategy;[62] the hymns are even more self-refer-
ential than the Qumran texts, talking about what they are doing.[63] This
shift in content makes the ascent of the reciter more obvious to the reader
than in the *Songs.*[64] While the *Songs* link the reciter of the liturgy with the
heavenly cult, the hekhalot hymns make him more directly part of the ac-

59. Maier, for example, delineates a distinct "hekhalot style" that includes the accumulation of verbs or nouns, the extension or elaboration of series of words, and the litanies of a
noun repeated with varying adjectives (1973). The difference between accumulation, repetition, extension, and elaboration is not clear. For Maier these structural elements are a sub-
set of the general structure of rabbinic prayer, which in turn is defined as combining rhythm,
loose parallelism, and the use of construct pairs to designate nouns.

60. Prose lines that look like complete sentences alternate with and merge into shorter
praise phrases that look more poetic. Hence Alexander's judicious conclusion that "the large
structures of the Heikhalot liturgies are formally ill-defined" (1987a:53). What coherence of
structure there is exists in the smaller units, because, as Alexander states, "rigorous symme-
try occurs only in the micro-forms" (1987a:53). See his careful review of Carmi's attempt
(1981) to make *Hekhalot Rabbati* par. 159–60 into stanzas (Alexander 1987a).

61. Newsom notes the complete lack of cited praise (1985:16).

62. Martha Himmelfarb (1988, 1993) limits technique to imperative verb forms (for example, "show the seal," "recite" names). Imperative verb forms are not however coextensive
with technique; they stand out because they are taught by means of direct order (hence the
modality of speech) and not by example. Similarly, Schäfer finds scant evidence of ritual
techniques in the texts, stating "The hekhalot literature does not provide us any indication
as to how the heavenly journey actually is carried out, or even if it is practiced at all as a
'truly' ecstatic experience" (1992:155).

63. Newsom notes that the hymns do not claim that the human priests conduct or participate in the heavenly cult (1990b:114). Thus they talk about what other beings are doing.
The closest overlap is the general action of praising.

64. And less controversial among scholars. The role of reciting praise to join the human
chorus to the heavenly chorus was noted as far back as Bloch 1893 and Altmann 1946, although the mechanisms were not explained.

tion by expanding the link to another dimension.[65] The recitation of angelic praise by the individual indexes him directly as a participant in the
heavenly chorus and not just a spectator of heavenly cult. The literary device of quoted speech or, in this case, quoted praise shifts the praise of the
heavenly speaker to the earthly one.[66] The hymns literally embed the heavenly praise in the human's mouth, making the text iconic at another
level.[67]

The hymns include a few instances of the standard rabbinic blessing
formula "ברוך/blessed," as in "Blessed are you . . . ," in this case completed by the phrase "wise in secrets." The act of blessing the deity has
been called "the most conspicuous form of Jewish prayer" (M. Smith
1982:203). Declaring the deity blessed is what the angelic choruses do; the
appropriation of this action by humans brings heavenly efficacy to earthly
requests. The rabbinic blessing formula summarizes the specific role of the
deity addressed in the prayers, in this case the deity is "wise in secrets."
The blessing formula includes a divine name and its recitation, and so is
restricted in use. The formula is awkward in that it includes both a third-
person description of the deity as blessed, and use of the second person
("you"). This phrasing permits the formula both to declare that the deity
is blessed and to instantiate the deity's presence as audience.[68] While this
enigmatic formula is worth noting because of its common occurrence in
rabbinic liturgy, in this text the few appearances of the formulas are an-
cillary to the main thrust of the text.

65. In more technical linguistic terms, this move completes a trajectory toward fully reflexive calibration across the human and divine realm.

66. In other hekhalot texts, we are overhearing a report of a successful ascent where, due
to the automatically effective language, the didactic role and the experiential role collapse
into one (Janowitz 1989).

67. Himmelfarb stresses the similarity between the hekhalot hymns and the synagogue
liturgy in order to negate any sense that the hekhalot hymns have any ritual efficacy. This
comparison does not negate the role of the hymns in ascent, but it does remind us that we
have not explained the role and purpose of the more common liturgy. With great insight she
remarks, "The hekhalot literature is intended for an audience of potential ascenders who
need to know the right words to say to be like angels" (1988:77). We are trying to explain
how the right words make someone like an angel.

68. As Heinemann noted in his extensive discussion of the formula, "One of the hall-
marks of the liturgical *berakah* in the statutory prayers is the address of God in the second
person, especially in the 'introductory clause' . . . although the 'main content clause' usually
continues in the third person. . . . The style is awkward, for the liturgical berakah uses the

In addition to fusing the reciter with the heavenly chorus, the hymns include the special power of divine names and letters with no clear distinction between the two.[69] Divine names occur less often in this text than in some of the other hekhalot texts.[70] The power of the divine name is also used in the ascent in the guise of angel names that derive from it. The recitation of divine names has stringent taboos, as seen in the fight that Rabbi Azariah has with Rabbi Nehunya when the latter fails to give the names of the angels in the seventh heaven. Nehunya explains that these names "have the name of the King of the world in them"—that is, they end with "אל/god"—and therefore Nehunya does not want to say them aloud.[71] However, the ascent is incomplete without them, so he finishes the list. There is no successful completion of the ascent without the recitation of the names, and no recitation of the seventh-heaven names without completion of the ascent.

The power of names is illustrated in a slightly different fashion in paragraph 204, where Ishmael is told that if he calls on Suria, the prince of the countenance, and vows a complex name of the deity 112 times, "immediately he descends and has power over the chariot." Here the names appear to be a functional equivalent to the recitation of hymns. The section is a

---

word *baruch* (blessed) in an adjectival sense, and not as a verb. Grammatically, then, it cannot be followed by a prepositional phrase." In order to explain these anomalies, Heinemann argued that the formula did not originally include the "you." The formula is a fusing of the form "Bless God who . . ." with "Blessed is God," as the latter became the hallmark of blessing (1977:100). He writes: "The same attributes of praise in the active participial form which were gleaned from the Bible came to serve a number of different liturgical functions. They were combined, as stated above, with the introductory formula '*Baruch Atah Adonay*,' and in this manner the new pattern of the *berakah* was created. . . . A pattern is needed in which the praise will be voiced in the present tense, and for this purpose the new pattern, in which the 'specific praise' is phrased in the form of an active participle, is most appropriate" (1977:91–93) (see Schlüter 1985).

69. Sometimes the text reads either "letter" or "letters" instead of a name. See Grozinger 1987:54.

70. See Schäfer 1992:140 n. 2. In the ascent hymns in *Ma'aseh Merkabah* the power of the divine name more directly supplies the "fuel" for the ascent. See Janowitz 1989. Some manuscripts (NY 8128) include more names, as if the copyist had a special preference for this technique.

71. This is very useful and clear articulation of the basis of the pragmatic implications of signs—that is, a metapragmatic statement. The revelation functions as an aside, and perhaps was added at some point by an editor who believed it was necessary to teach explicitly the principles that other parts of the text teach by example.

conscious reflection on ascent techniques, incorporating ascent as one more task that can be accomplished by calling on angels.[72]

Once in the heavenly realm, Nehunya shows seals to the gatekeepers on the left and the right in order to pass from one level to the next.[73] The practice of using seals is referred to in several *hekhalot* texts.[74] Sealing is not so much an ascent technique as a protective device used to negotiate the heavens once in the heavenly realm. The Orphians, according to Origen, show "symbols" as they pass through the levels of heaven (*Against Celsus* 6.27). In the *Ascension of Isaiah* 10.24 the angels at the heavenly gates demand to see a "character." Showing a seal proves to the heavenly beings that the individual is protected by the highest powers and permits him to pass to the next level.[75] In many cases, the seals appear to include the divine name, incorporating yet another icon of the name into the ritual.[76] It is also possible that a seal consists of letters of the divine names, as we saw with the spoken permutations of divine names.

In the ascent rituals, the term "seal" may refer to amulets worn by the practitioner, as noted by Morton Smith (1963) and argued most recently by Rebecca Lesses (1998:319).[77] Another intriguing possibility is that sealing refers to writing directly on the body.[78] It is often impossible to tell

---

72. See the discussion in Chapter 6 about employing angels.

73. Scholem notes that the Hebrew term is parallel to the Greek term *sphragis* (1965a:133). For a general review of the imagery of seals, see Fitzer 1971, and for a discussion of seals in the hekhalot texts, see Lesses 1998:317–23.

74. *Ma'aseh Merkabah* 23, 3 Enoch 48d:5.

75. For sealing as means of gaining protection, see *Merkabah Rabba,* where the practitioner seals himself and asks for mercy (709).

76. The *Book of Jeu* states, "Tell the mystery, and seal yourself with this seal, this is his name" (*GCS* 13.315–21). According to rabbinic legend, God's amulet is the "greatest" version of the divine name—that is, the Torah.

77. In the Naasene hymn Jesus prays, "For his salvation send me, that I may go down with the seals in my hands, traverse all the aeons, open all the mysteries, disclose all divine beings to him, and proclaim to him the secret of the holy way—I call it knowledge" (Hippolytus *Refutation of All Heresies* 5.10). For other examples, see Lesses 1998:318.

78. In addition to the rabbinic texts cited below, a dream revelation from the Genizah instructs the practitioner to write divine names on his left hand (Lesses 1998:318). Bar-Ilan argues that by writing on his skin the practitioner makes himself into a slave of the deity (1989:44). This practice is also mentioned in a Coptic spell (Lesses 1998:318 n. 212). Another practice of "sealing" directly on the flesh is anointing the body with oil. According to Rudolph the protective property of the sealing is related to the paradisical olive tree, with which the oil is equated (1983:228, 361).

whether the seals are amulets or letters written directly on the body; very possibly both methods were combined.[79] The practice of writing divine names directly on the body is attested in several places in rabbinic literature (Bar-Ilan 1989). Seen through the rabbinic lens, all sorts of potential problems emerge from the practice. For example, mYoma 8:3 debates whether a man who has written on his limbs may bathe or stand in an impure place. mMaccot 3:6 states that a man is not liable for "marking his flesh" unless he writes the name—that is, the name of God. Some rabbis are presented as opposing the practice (tMaccot 4:15), which other texts appear to take for granted.

Writing names on one's body is a rich semiotic practice; the names in themselves are powerful, and that power is transferred directly to the person's marked body.[80] The human body becomes an icon of the divine body with its named limbs. Once marked with the name, the human body looks even more like the divine body, which as we saw in the last chapter was understood to have names on each limb. Any special mark on the flesh could be interpreted as a name, and thus a seal. Even the mark of circumcision, interpreted as the adding of a letter from the divine name to the flesh, could seal and thus protect a man.[81]

The goal of the ascent in *Hekhalot Rabbati* is a slippery question. Numerous possibilities have been suggested, including a foretaste of the heavenly world (Scholem 1965a:17–18), the pursuit of Torah-knowledge (Halperin 1988:366–87), gaining the protection of the heavenly court,[82] and attempting to "storm heaven" or participate in the heavenly praise and thus achieve "unio liturgica" (Schäfer 1992:152–53). Many of the more general explanations, such as the compensatory role of ascent in the face of the loss of the Temple or of life under the Romans, fail to take into account the widespread occurrence of the phenomenon in the Late Antique world.

It is easy to shift the goal of ascent by adding a new introduction to a

---

79. Note the ambiguity in the phrases in the Aramaic additions to *Ma'aseh Merkabah* where the practitioner fasts and then seals himself, reciting the phrase "seal on my limbs" (par. 566). Later in the text he again states, "There will be a seal on all my limbs" (par. 569).

80. The Golem was vivified when the divine name was inscribed on his forehead.

81. See tBer 6:24, jBer 9:3, bShabbat 137b, and the discussion by Wolfson 1987.

82. Alexander 1987a:77, based on *Hekhalot Rabbati* secs. 1.1–2.21.

text. Whatever its original goal, the ascent in *Hekhalot Rabbati* has been reedited into a new frame.[83] This frame, which includes the first several paragraphs of the text, promises that the ascent hymns will enable the reciter to "see the deeds of men" and to know what the future holds. With this frame the ascent is itself redirected to new goals. The ability to work the cosmology, going up and down at will, becomes a tool that permits the ascender to achieve a myriad of decidedly this-worldly goals. The multiuse idea is built into *Hekhalot Rabbati* when Nehunya says that knowing the ritual is like having a ladder in one's home.

The description of Rabbi Nehunya's ascent shares many elements with other Greco-Roman ascent texts. In particular, Morton Smith compared *Hekhalot Rabbati* with the *Mithras Liturgy,* found in an early fourth-century Greek papyrus.[84] The *Liturgy* follows a soul on a journey through the heavens, and the ascent in the *Liturgy* combines recitation of prayers and cosmic sounds with breathing techniques and kissing amulets; the efficacy of the rite is dependent on the combination of all these actions. While the general strategies overlap with the hekhalot ascent, the structuring of the ritual illuminates the contrasts.[85]

The *Mithras Liturgy* has a distinct tone, described by Tabor as "a journey into the self beholding of the immortal nature beyond the bounds of mortality and Fate" (1986:93). The ascent begins with a prayer combining letter sounds with creation imagery: "First origin of my origin, AEEIOYO,[86] first beginning of my beginning, PPP SSS PHR[E]" (4.487–88). The prayer includes references to the building blocks of the created world—spirit, fire, and water—elements that are located "within me" as the reciter is identified with the cosmos. The reciter has now been "born again in thought" (4.510), a new birth better than his first one. Positing a

---

83. The ascent is introduced directly by the story of an impending persecution by Rome. Similarly, in one of the three apocalypses near the start of the text, Israel is protected from Roman persecution by the replacement of the Caesar by Rabbi Teradyon. The story is then placed in yet another frame, this one directed toward divination.

84. Papyrus 574 of the Bibliothèque Nationale, *PGM* 4.475–829.

85. For a comparison of the *Mithras Liturgy* with an ascent ritual in the *Chaldean Oracles,* see Johnston 1997.

86. Because Hebrew is written without vowels, divine names and cosmic sounds are going to be strings of consonants and not vowels. When Jewish texts are written in Greek, the same emphasis on vowels appears in them as well.

new origin and a new beginning is a clever strategy for a text that seeks to alter bodily existence and create an immortal person (Janowitz 1991).

Recitation of strings of letters equated with cosmic elements incorporates their transformative power into the prayers ("and the sacred spirit may breath in me, NECHTHEN APOTOU NECHTHIN ARPI ETH" [4.510]). The individual is then instructed to "draw in breath from the rays, drawing up three times as much as you can, and you will see yourself being lifted up and ascending to the height, so that you seem to be in mid-air" (4.539–40). These breathing techniques, including the making of hissing and popping sounds, enable the ascender to take off and begin his travel through the cosmos. He is able to see "himself" as he separates his soul from his body.[87]

Once traveling toward the upper regions, the ascender tries to pass himself off as a star—that is, as a natural inhabitant of the heavens (4.570–75). The process depends in part on identification, with the individual literally redefining himself as a cosmic being by reciting "I am a star" (4.574). In the heavenly realm, he receives a guide to help him (4.630–60). In this case, the gatekeeper is a young god from whom the ascender asks protection. More breathing techniques dot the continuing passage upward, along with references to kissing amulets. "And at once produce a long bellowing sound, straining your belly, that you may excite the five senses: bellow long until the conclusions, and again kiss the amulets and say . . ." (4.704–8). The practitioner begins to lose his sense of self, saying, "I am passing away" (4.721), until the reciter is told, "Now you will grow weak in soul and will not be in yourself" (4.725).

A striking parallel to this ritual strategy is found in the Nag Hammadi tractate *Marsanes,* where an ascent is achieved by a combination of recitation of hymns, silences, the invocation of names, and the recitation of strings of vowels (Pearson 1984). The text combines for us the use of vowels with some of the philosophy of language articulated in the Neoplatonic texts, with vowels said to be the "shapes" of the souls (25*1–26*12, 27*23–30*2). In particular, spherical shapes are associated with the seven vowels (25*1–26*12).[88]

---

87. The parallel bi-locations in *Hekhalot Rabbati* are noted above.

88. Pearson relates this to the speculation in Timaeus 35A–36A (1981). He also notes the work of Dionysius Thrax as discussed by Böhlig and Wisse 1975:16–17.

The numerous instructions in the *Mithras Liturgy* result in the more tentative mood of the text than in *Hekhalot Rabbati*. They introduce actions that are referred to (draw in, produce), and mention props that must be correctly used (amulets). Teaching is done by talking about action, because the actions are not only verbal. The ritual therefore has less of the "automatic" quality of *Hekhalot Rabbati*. The phrasing of the text is not the tight didactic structure of *Hekhalot Rabbati* in which Rabbi Nehunya simultaneously teaches and ascends. The combinations of types of actions employed in the *Mithras Liturgy* preclude such a didactic structure. In addition to the need to include instructions, the constant shift between first and second person sets up a distinction between the instructions to say a prayer (You say X) and the content of the prayers (in the first person). For example, specific heavenly greetings for each constellation are spoken in the first person and interlaced with strings of vowels.[89] The numerous imperative forms, "Draw up breath" and so on, also distinguish the person teaching from the one attempting the ascent. Again this points to a different didactic structure, in which the teaching of the ritual can be separated from its use. The hekhalot texts, at least in terms of the ascent materials,[90] are characterized by the collapsing of teaching into experiencing, a structure that is inseparable from the internal theory of language with its automatic efficacy.

The *Mithras Liturgy* is more explicit about its goal than *Hekhalot Rabbati,* stating directly that the process confers immortality. The text begins with a direct request: "For an only child, I request immortality" (4.476). The invocation includes a call to "give me over to immortal birth" (4.501), and the hailing formula declares that the reciter has become immortal (4.647).[91] Quite an astonishing array of rituals were thought to confer divinity, and ascent was one of them.[92] Nock considered the

89. Other letter strings are made up entirely of vowels, a technique that is absent from the hekhalot texts because Hebrew is written without vowels.

90. The hekhalot texts include a variety of materials beyond ascents. For example, the Prince of the Torah (Sar Ha-Torah) rituals attempt to manifest this particular divine figure in order to gain his assistance. The structure of these rituals is distinct, with explicit instructions about fasting and other actions.

91. See the remark by Proclus that ascent brings immortality (*Commentary on the Republic* 1.152.10).

92. See Nock 1966:54 nn. 70–71.

Liturgy a ritual means for achieving divinity while still alive, as opposed to the notion that divinity is regained only after death.[93]

As a ritual geared toward making someone immortal, the *Mithras Liturgy* was probably originally meant to effect a one-time transformation. The ritual has been reedited and directed toward divination, much as the *Shi'ur Komah* materials were reedited. Like the ascent in *Hekhalot Rabbati,* this ascent also has additions that appear before the ascent, and appended instructions for supplemental rituals.[94]

Whatever the purpose, ascent was believed to be achieved by means of identification with the heavenly world, and in particular by means of the repetition of heavenly sounds. In the tremendously plastic rituals of ascent we see the process by which humans, either for a moment or for eternity, become something other than their regular selves. Learning to "talk" like the heavens produces a set of audible signs that point back to the speaker; he is now someone who has changed his status and can operate both on earth and in heaven. We should not be fooled by the stereotypical content of the words he utters, for they are more powerful than any and all earthly words.

93. For recovering divinity after death, Nock cites Orphic inscriptions and the gold leaf found in tombs.

94. An introductory reference to herbs and spices is usually considered an addition. The end of the text includes instructions for a scarab ceremony and for making amulets, with two additional compositions appended.

6

COMBINING WORDS AND DEEDS: ANGELIC IMPRECATIONS IN THE *Book of Secrets*

T he *Book of Secrets* is the classic example for modern scholars of Late Antique Jewish "magic."[1] The word "magic" does not occur in the text, though English translations sometimes insert the word.[2] The text is a collection of approximately twenty-nine recipes[3] for a miscellany of tasks ranging from how to make a wall collapse to how to question a ghost (see Table 1). The collection has the form of a handbook, similar to the ritual handbooks found in the Greek papyri.[4] In this collection serious requests for healing are combined with the seemingly comic, such as one recipe promising to fill a room up with smoke in order to impress friends. All the tasks are accomplished with the help of angels obtained by means of imprecations and complex recipes.[5]

---

1. Modern scholars who label the text "magic" include most scholars who write about this text: Schäfer (1990), Morgan (1983), Margalioth (1966), Niggemeyer (1975), Dan (1967–68), Gruenwald (1980:225–34), Maier (1968a), and Swartz (1990). The only exceptions I have found are Merchavya (1967), who stresses its "mystical" aspect, and Kasher (1967), who argues, using rabbinic criteria, that the text is theoretical and not strictly magical. The *Book of Secrets* is cited by formula number followed by the number of the heaven and line number in the Morgan translation (1983). Thus, #28 (5.15) refers to formula #28 from Table 1, which appears in the fifth heaven beginning on line 15.

2. See, for example, Morgan's translation of "עסק/practice" as "practice magic," and "מעשה/occurrence" as "magical rite" (1983:21).

3. Several of the recipes are composites that can be counted singly or as a cluster of formulas. Similarly, in the *Greek Magical Papyri* (*PGM*) a series of partial recipes is combined so that it is difficult to tell how many separate rituals are involved.

4. See, for example, *PGM*, nos. 1, 3, 4, 5, 7, 12, 13, and 36. Morton Smith differentiates these collections from individual formulas either written for specific persons or with no references to specific people (1979:129 n. 4).

5. Morton Smith estimates that 70 percent of the *PGM* papyri concern the use of such helpers and projects they can complete (1986:68).

In order to understand these recipes and their perceived efficacy, we need to look beyond the techniques examined thus far, though some elements will be familiar. The recipes combine the recitation of verbal formulas, including divine names, with a series of actions, some familiar and some rather exotic. Most important for this analysis, we shall see how the use of words and objects establish exact models of the goals toward which the rituals are directed, encoding in them the purpose of the ritual. Just as we found that words can "do things," the combined use of objects is related to culturally specific notions of effective actions.

The *Book of Secrets*[6] is written in a very literate Hebrew with a few instances of transliterated Greek. The modern editor Margalioth reconstructed the text from five main manuscripts, supplemented by readings from genizah fragments, Latin and Arabic manuscripts.[7] This fact has been used to challenge the integrity of the text and to argue that it is simply the construction of its modern editor. Just as in the case of the *hekhalot* texts, the controversial nature of the material has led to unusually close scrutiny of the textual traditions. This question must be viewed within the standards for other texts. The textual history is no more daunting than that of other Late Antique manuals, such as, for example, Apicius' cookbook (Brandt 1927).

In the case of the *Book of Secrets* we lack the paleographical evidence helpful in dating similar Greek texts (Morgan 1983:8). Dating the text is based in part on a single reference to Roman indiction in section 1.27–28 ("the fifteen year cycle of the reckoning of the Greek kings"). This system was instituted in the year 312 (Margalioth 1966:24–25) but was not used in nonfiscal contexts until the second half of the fourth century.[8] The single reference can be supplemented by general comparisons with Greek papyri that point to a date from the early third century to the late fourth century.

---

6. This may not have been its original title. See Margalioth 1966:56–62 and Merchavya 1971:1594, who posits that the book may have been named after the angel Raziel or Noah.

7. For the manuscript evidence, see Margalioth (1966:47–55) and Morgan (1983:2–6). For a depiction of the relationship between the various sources, see the chart in Niggemeyer (1975) between pages 18 and 19.

8. Alexander (1986:348 n. 15) supplements Margalioth's discussion, adding that the indiction method of counting years began in 312, with a five-year indiction in Egypt perhaps as early as 287. However, Alexander notes that the use of this method in "non-fiscal contexts" did not begin until the second half of the fourth century (following Bickerman 1980:78). If the text is unitary, this date helps place the entire composition.

The text is bound with *merkabah/hekhalot* (chariot/palace) treatises in five of the six main manuscript copies (*Ma'aseh Hekhalot, Ma'aseh Bereshit,* and *Shi'ur Komah*) and shares many of their cosmological conceptions, such as descriptions of the heavenly realm as the world of fiery angels who recite endless praise of the deity.[9] The text is structured in seven distinct sections, each one corresponding with a heavenly level and each containing a number of imprecations.[10] The heavenly framework enumerates the names of the angels in that heaven, their mode of organization, the tasks over which they are appointed, and how they can be employed in the various tasks. The seventh and final section of the framework, the seventh heaven, consists entirely of extensive hymns similar to the *hekhalot* hymns.

The formulas appear in the heavens in no clear progression, other than a steady decrease in the number of recipes per heaven.[11] This is true of the parallel Greek ritual handbooks (*PGM*) as well, where the organization of recipes is not clear. The range of the ritual goals is striking, combining very serious rituals with seemingly comic ones.[12] Both these aspects of the text are also familiar from parallel Greek texts.[13]

9. The section on the seventh heaven in the *Book of Secrets* appears at the end of *Sefer HaQommah* in one manuscript. See Morgan 1983:2 and Margalioth 1966:xv.

10. Morgan and other commentators view the recipes as a composition distinct from the heavenly framework, with disagreement about which is earlier. Morgan (1983:9, 27) notes that the recipes lack the "flowery descriptive wording and the biblical quotations of the cosmological framework" and posits that the recipes were composed first and the cosmological framework added later. Merchavya argues the reverse (1971:1594–95). However, distinct wordings for the adjurations and the hymns does not mean they were written by different authors. Alexander points out that the angel names occur both in the recipes and in the descriptions of the heavens, forming an important link between the sections (1986:347–48). The recipes also refer directly to the framework, with this interweaving making it difficult to draw a distinct line between frame and recipe.

11. Healing appears in different sections; #1 (1.29) is a general healing formula, #17 (2.95) is for stroke, and #23 (2.182) is for curing a headache or blindness. Both #3 (1.94) and #28 (5.15) are for knowing about the future.

12. Compare the recipe for making a room fill up with smoke to impress friends (#26) with the recipe for making men appear to have donkey snouts (*PGM* 11b:1–5).

13. As a few examples, compare the ritual for binding lovers (5.13) with *PGM* 4:296–466, knowing the future (#28) with some of the many divination rituals such as *PGM* 4:3210 and 7:540–78, the prayers to Helios (#27B with *PGM* 4:247), and the making of amulets (#18), with an amulet for a pregnant woman *PGM* 4:80.

Table 1. Outline of the *Book of Secrets*

No.	Placement/Purpose	Action / (Ma'aseh)	Utterances
		First Firmament	
1st Encampment:			
1	Heal (29)	Burn incense (S)	Angel names, request formula
2nd Encampment:			
2	Against enemy, creditor etc. (composite) (29)	Gather water in vessels; smash vessels (A)	Request formulas
3rd Encampment:			
3	Know future (94)	Put written slips in oil	Adjuration (sun)
4th Encampment:			
4A	Influence king (117)	Take heart of lion cub; write angel names with blood/incense (S)	Angel names, adjuration to Aphrodite
4B	Enter presence of king (132)	Anoint self with 4A mixture; hide lion's heart (S)	Request formula
5	Bind yourself to great woman (143)	Take your sweat; bury flask under her doorstep (A)	Adjuration
5th Encampment:			
6A	To speak to moon/stars (161)	Kill cock, make cakes, write angel names (S)	Angel names, adjuration or formula
6B	Kindness to you (170)	Put cakes in wine (S)	Angel names, adjuration
7	Question ghost (175)	Face tomb, hold oil and honey (S)	Angel names, adjuration to Hermes, release formula
8	Speak with spirits (187)	Go to place of killed	Adjuration (singsong)
6th Encampment:			
9	(Catch a fugitive) (202)	Write his name (A)	Request formula

7th Encampment:

	Go to riverbank, incense (S)	Angel names, adjuration, release formulas
10 Answer king (217)		
	Second Firmament	
11 Ask anything of angels in second firmament (6)	Abstain	—
12 Silence powerful people (18)	Ashes from idol bread offering (S/A)	Angel names backward Request formulas
13 Make woman love man (30)	Lamellae with angel names	Request formula put in furnace or her bath
14 Nullify great man's intention to you (46)	Stand at midnight	Angel name, request formula
15 Give enemy trouble sleeping (62)	Head of black dog, amulet with angel names (S)	Request formula hide head-with-amulet near him (release: remove and burn)
16 Light an oven in the cold (81)	Write angels names on sulfur lump, put in oven (A)	Adjuration
17 Heal a man with stroke (95)	Apply oil, honey to him, burn incense, amulet (S/A)	Patient's name Angel names
18 Expel lion, etc. (111)	Make image, amulet, bury/place it (A)	
19 For childbirth (124)	Amulets (on house, woman)	—
20 Protect man in war (134)	Write angel names on leaves, put in oil, anoint him, amulet (S/A)	—
21 Rescue friend from bad judgment (145)	Purify self, amulet	Request formula
22 Restore to office (161)	Oil, honey, flour in vial, make cake, he eats it (S/A)	Angel names Adjuration (to moon)
23 Cure headache/blindness (182)	Brain of black ox, write, angel names, amulet, abstain (S)	—

Third Firmament			
24	Extinguish bathhouse fire (17)	Put salamander in jar with oil (A)	Adjuration (Salamander)
25	Race horses (36)	Hide amulet in track	Adjuration
26	Give proof of your powers, to fill room with smoke (47)	Burn plant (S)	Adjuration (reverse: adjuration backward with addition)
Fourth Firmament			
27A	View sun during day, be pure (25)	Abstain, incense	Angel names, adjuration
27B	See sun during night (43)	Purify, abstain, wear white, bow	Name of sun, angel names, adjuration, prayer to Helios (release: adjuration)
Fifth Firmament			
28	Know future (15)	Put lamellae on oil	Adjuration 7 times
Sixth Firmament			
29	For journey or to war, to flee, etc. (composite) (25)	Make iron ring, lamellae with angel names in ring, put in mouth (A)	Angel names, adjuration

S = modified sacrifice
A = analogical action

Verbal Formulas

The majority of the verbal formulas in the first six heavens are adjurations[14] with first-person singular forms of "מַשְׁבִּיעַ/adjure, swear" (Table 1,
column 3).[15] Examples include "I adjure you angels of wrath and destruction (1.70) and "I adjure you O sun that shines on the earth (1.99). This
verb parallels closely the Greek verb "ὁρκίζω/swear," found throughout
Greek ritual texts.[16] The range of adjurations—Greek, Hebrew, Coptic,
and Demotic—reflects the widespread trope that humans can gain angelic
assistants.[17] A major complex of these rituals occurs in the *hekhalot* texts,
many of the rituals directed at gaining help from the Prince of the Torah
(שר התורה).[18]

Angelic adjurations are a subcategory of the much more widespread
social practice of swearing and adjuring. Oaths were most familiar in the
Greco-Roman world, from the area of law. An oath would be taken when
signing a treaty, setting up a commercial contract or a personal contract,
for marriages, and for swearing in officials of the government and sol-

---

14. No. 2, 1.68, 1.70; #3, 1.98; #4, 1.126; #5, 1.146; #6, 1.172; #7, 1.179; #8, 1.189;
#10, 1.226; #16, 2.83; #22, 2.166; #24, 3.20, 3.28; #25, 3.38; #26, 3.52, #27A, 4.30, 4.41;
#27B, 4.68; #28, 5.23; #29, 6.35.

15. The only extended stylistic analysis of the formulas is Niggemeyer's work (1975),
which is limited by its formulaic distinction between "prayers" and "magical language." His
analysis defines a prayer as a petition plus a request, while a "swearing" is a petition plus a
magical binding formula. To no surprise, he then finds that the addition of a "swearing formula" makes a "prayer" into "magical language." If the distinctions (prayers, swearing formula) are simply definitional, then the analysis is completely tautological. Otherwise the
import of this terminology is not made clear. Niggemeyer finds a few cases where names appear in what otherwise should, according to his nomenclature, be a prayer. These usages are
explained as being prayer on its way to magical language, another conclusion completely de-
termined by the initial organization of the terms. In his final section, Niggemeyer lists twelve
elements of magical speech, ranging from the use of specific types of words such as names,
to vague categories, such as "exactitude of language" and "modalities." He does not explain
the functions of the elements. Perhaps Niggemeyer is hindered in general by a hesitancy to
see the use of hostile language as part of religious practice. The imprecations try to convince
angels to harm people, and thus do not fit easily into everyone's picture of proper religious
language. See, for example, Alan Segal's comment about the use of curses tablets: "No one
would have practiced it with the impression he was practicing a legal and wholesome religious rite, however richly deserved was the damage to the intended victim" (1981:88–97).

16. See, for example, the numerous instances in the *PGM*, such as 1.134.

17. See the extended discussion in Lesses 1998:279–365.

18. As Michael Swartz has argued, these rituals are distinct from the ascent rites and may
be later additions (1996).

diers, and even by doctors (Hippocratic Oath). A wide variety of deities could be invoked in these oaths, with Greeks often referring to the triad of sky, earth, and sea gods, and Romans swearing by Jupiter or simply by "all the gods" (Dillon 1996:1057).

This practice was also common among Late Antique Jews (Lieberman 1974: esp. 24). For example the Hebrew phrase "I adjure you and may it come upon you" combines an oath and a curse (tSota 2:1; bSota 18a). Adjurations were made invoking the deity, as in the phrase "by He who established the world on three pillars" (*Song of Songs Rabba* 7.8)[19] or directly by the divine name.[20] Such adjurations were often employed in a time of trouble or stress.

In addition to the adjurations, ritual formulas in the *Book of Secrets* contain a variety of other verbs—for example, "I ask you angels . . ." (#12, 2.21–23) and "I charge you angels . . ." (#9, 1.203) (labeled "request formulas" in Table 1, column 3).[21] Almost all these formulas preserve the first-person verb form[22] and are addressed to a specific group of angels, such as "angels of fury," or to individual angels, such as the sun (#27B, 4.61). The ancient editor made no clear distinction between the adjurations and the request formulas. For example, the goal of speaking to the moon or stars can be reached using either type (#6A, 1.165 and 1.167).[23] Given the preponderance of adjurations, the other formulas appear to assimilate as a subclass of adjurations.

All these verbal formulas reflect a distinct mode of language function. Working with angels involves a search for the best authority to bring to bear on the subject, and the approach used here, which presumably res-

---

19. See also *Song of Songs Rabba* 7.9 and Lieberman 1965a:107–8; 1974:24.

20. For an example of an adjuration made "by the Name" transliterated into Greek, see *PGM* 2.110, and see tNedarim 1:1, which states that "in the name" is an oath. Alon 1950:33 and Albeck 1952:470.

21. See "I ask you angels" (#13, 2.33), "I request you, great angel" (#21, 2.147), and "I present my supplication before you" (#27B, 4.64). In a few cases, the speaker states that he is turning a certain person over to the angels so that they will punish him. "I deliver to you . . . so that you will strangle . . ." (#2, 1.64).

22. Slight variations are found in "You angels . . . let the terror of me be over . . ." (#4B, 1.136), "Moon moon, moon . . . bring my words before the angels" (#6A, 1.162), and one case of an angel name followed by "accept from my hand what I throw to you" (#2, 1.57).

23. Similarly, in the *PGM* adjuration formulas are mixed in with formulas that use other nonadjuring verbs.

onates well with our culture, is to "threaten to sue." The thrust of the formulas is to put the angels in a situation in which they cannot refuse to help the person making the request. They can no more pretend that they did not hear the request than someone can ignore a summons.

Angels and daimons were thought to exert far-reaching influence on daily life, and life was lived keeping one eye on their activities.[24] Complex social networks of responsibilities and obligations extended from the human world to the supernatural so that angels could be addressed using the same linguistic forms as humans. In the *Book of Secrets,* the speaker addresses an angel with an oath cast as forcefully as possible in the first person, the use of the second-person addressee indexing the presence of the angel as intended audience/receiver. The practitioner must know the names of angels and their taxonomy (which angel does what and works for whom), all outlined extensively in the text.

Adjuring angels as a legal mode of discourse suggests the degree to which it was a socially recognized activity. We are in the realm of very specialized ways of talking that are calibrated with social roles. The person using the adjuration is presumably at the same social level as the angels he adjures. The adjurations also incorporate the power of divine names, because angel names include the letters "el/god."

An illustrative use of the legal adjuration appears in a rabbinic story about Rabbi Joshua ben Levi adjuring the angel of death (bKetubot 77b).[25] When the angel gives him a tour and permits him a premature glimpse of paradise, the rabbi jumps down into paradise and refuses to go back and die. He adjures the angel so that angel will not be able to take him back. As always in rabbinic stories, the point of the story is about something else (in this case the importance of fulfilling one's vows); the reference to the adjuring of the angel is off-hand and without controversy. The context here is of a struggle between near equals, a battle of wits and words in which the rabbi can overcome the natural order (die first, then paradise) if his adjuration works.[26]

24. For the widespread belief in daimons, see, among others, M. Smith 1978:126–29, 202–5, and Neusner 1966–70, 4:334–441, 440; 5:183–86, 217–43.

25. In some versions it is R. Johanan. See Lieberman 1974:24.

26. Typically rabbinic, another discussion of oaths states that an adjuration is binding only if the one adjured accepts it (bShevuot 29b).

The use of adjurations contrasts with other ritual strategies for influencing lower-level supernatural beings, such as use of imperatives or even having a completely distinct "daimon" language. The latter is found, for example, in the "language of the demons" of mantras, which Tambiah argues "is muttered by the exorcist and . . . is not meant to be heard, for it constitutes secret knowledge" (1985:19). Instead of conveying information, the words "connote power" (1985:20).

In the *Book of Secrets,* the only formula with a special intonation is the one addressed to spirits who dwell in a place where people are killed. Such places were believed to be especially replete with spirits of people who either died before their time or were killed violently. These spirits were thought to linger near their graves, and thus be accessible to the living (Waszink 1950). The officiant is told to speak in a "singsong" voice, a tone that may be related to the common notion that supernatural spirits whisper (tShabbat 7.23). Other than that, neither special languages nor special intonation looms large in the *Book of Secrets;* instead, the primary mode of talking with an angel employs legal language.

The relentless focus of the recipes is not on the person being healed or subject to attack; the formulas are all addressed to angelic helpers. The formulas have to fulfill two purposes at the same time; they must be persuasive to the angel and they must convey sufficient information about the goal to direct the angelic power. As such, they are complex mediating formulas, mediating both between the human speaker and the angel and between the human speaker and his goal. As such they also differ from Greek binding spells, formulas inscribed on small sheets of metal and placed in tombs, chthonic sanctuaries, and, later, near bodies of water or even in hippodromes (Faraone 1991). These spells have goals (personal and financial success) that are similar to the recipes in the *Book of Secrets* but differ in their specific formulation: binding spells use direct formulations, such as "I bind NN," which do not occur in this text due to its relentless focus on getting angels to do the work.

Once in the seventh heaven, the officiant recites hymns. The recipes in the *Greek Magical Papyri (PGM)* also include numerous hymns, some of which are cast in archaic language (*PGM* 3:215). The hymns in the *Book of Secrets* praise the God who dwells on his exalted throne, concluding with some typical praise:

Blessed be his Name alone on his throne
And blessed in dwelling places of His majesty
Blessed be His name in the mouth of all living
And blessed in the song of every creature
Blessed be the Lord forever.

(7.39)

The distinction between the modes of discourse in the lower heavens and in the highest heaven is based on a clear hierarchy of language—that is, the mode of speaking relates to the status of the addressee (a standard sociolinguistic observation). All cultures have a range of ways of making requests, from the direct command "scalpel" to the maximally polite request to close a window by stating "My, it's cold in here" (Ervin-Tripp 1976).

Similarly, for practitioners of all stripes the plethora of supernatural powers inhabiting the cosmos demanded an etiquette that took into account their hierarchy; it was necessary to act appropriately with each type of supernatural figure. Adjurations were never to be used in relation to the main deity. Attacks could be made against any ritual that appeared to violate the expected etiquette. Raising one's voice, for example, or talking too directly to a deity was not considered proper etiquette. Prayer is better than other forms of discourse because it is understood to be a more polite form of address.[27] A raised voice should be reserved for lower-level spirits. Iamblichus, for example, explains to Porphyry that the Egyptians do not threaten their gods, only daimons (*On the Mysteries* 7.6).[28] On the other hand, adverse comments were made about being too sycophantic in relationship to the deity, as in the rabbinic texts that distinguish between those who flatter their deity too much (pagans) and the superior language of Jewish prayer (Lieberman 1974:25).

In the *Book of Secrets,* angelic adjurations are limited to the lower six heavens. At the top level there is no ordering of angels and no need to procure various artifacts. Striving to see the deity demands a higher-brow

---

27. See Irenaeus' statement that Christians use only pure, sincere prayer, not incantations (*Against the Heresies* 2.32.5).

28. Some modern scholars have reified Iamblichus' distinctions, which are based on etiquette, into substantive categories (religious versus requests versus magical threats).

mode of action than interacting with the lower powers. At the highest level the only language used is hymns, complete with their distinct practice of declaring the deity blessed. As noted in Chapter 5, the meaning and purpose of blessing the deity is not immediately clear.[29] As we saw in the ascent texts, the hymns in the seventh heaven are reported speech—that is, the speaker reports the speech of the biblical angelic chorus that declares the blessed status of the deity. Humans thus recycle the cosmic praise and mark their status as participants in the seventh heaven.

The fact that this level has no adjuration does not mean that no demands are made or that nothing is wanted from the deity.[30] In other words, the right to address someone respectfully can sometimes indicate certain expectations of the addressee. A recent study of politeness in Samoan respect language points out that use of respect language is not just a way of being nice, but also places demands on the person to whom the polite language is addressed. Duranti explains: "Respect is not only given in exchange for something (for example, request, imposition of various kinds), it is also a pragmatic force that coerces certain behaviors or actions upon people and thus indexes speakers' control over addresses rather than addressees' 'freedom' of action" (1992:96).[31] To declare one's deity blessed using the most polite forms may simply be the nicest way possible to make a request.[32] Being able to use the most polite form in the highest level also reflects the elevated status of the speaker.

29. Reif comments that blessing God "counts as another form of Jewish worship that continued from earlier times into the axial age" and posits that it is basically a mode of giving thanks (1993:60). See the comments on the berakah formulas above, in Chapter 6.

30. Recently Jon Levenson hints in a footnote that biblical prayers may be indirect requests. "There is room to wonder, however, whether those affirmations of God's continual solicitude, and protection of his loyal worshiper too, are not often theurgic rather than static and simply descriptive. My suspicion is that they often constitute a hopeful pledge of allegiance to YHWH's ideal reputation, rather than the Pollyannaish reporting of empirical fact that they seem to be" (1994:xxviii n. 12).

31. See the Concluding Note, at the end of this book, for further discussion of modes of requests.

32. In linguistic terms, this is a typology of demands with markedness proportional to register.

What Is a Ma'aseh? Modified Sacrifices and Analogies

The *Book of Secrets* does not contain any rituals that consist entirely of the recitation of words.[33] All the recipes combine verbal formulas with the use of objects; the composite recipes are called "מעשה (act/deed)." The use of the Hebrew term "act" is very close to the Greek "πρᾶχις (action/doing)," translated as "rite" in the recent English edition of the Greek ritual handbooks (Betz 1986).

Rabbinic texts mention a category of "men of deed," the most famous of whom is Honi the Circle-Drawer.[34] Honi was able to bring rain by standing inside a circle he drew and using an adjuration. His behavior is presented as being very audacious in the rabbinic texts. The combination of adjuration and standing inside a circle is similar to the rites in The *Book of Secrets*.

Many of the "rites" in this book involve more complicated actions than attributed to Honi. The officiant is told to procure and employ a variety of objects for use with the verbal recitations (Table 1, column 2). For example, the first recipe in the first heaven combines reciting a formula while burning incense. Objects needed for the various recipes range from the common (water, incense, and oil) to the more exotic (a lion-cub heart, the head of a black dog, the brain of a black ox). These objects are no more obscure than those employed in the parallel Greek rituals, one of which demands "fat of dappled goat, embryo of a dog and bloody discharge of a virgin dead untimely" (4.2645–46).[35]

Just as the verbal formulas include a number of persuasive devices, the ritual use of these objects is multilayered. The actions appear to fall into two categories: some are modified sacrifices that include, for example, the use of incense and blood, while others appear to be constructed as analogies to the desired outcomes of the rituals.[36]

33. There are a few examples of the reverse, where letters or words are written down and objects are manipulated with no oral recitation. These will be discussed below.

34. See mTa'anit 3:8, bTa'anit 19a, 23 ab, mSotah 9:5, *Genesis Rabba* 5.5, 13.7, and Bokser 1985:42.

35. The presence of these exotic items is part of the reason Merchavya (1966–67) considers the text a purely theoretical exercise.

36. Modified sacrifices are marked (S) and analogical actions are marked (A) in the second column of Table 1.

Looking at the former category first, some of the recipes include burning incense, making cakes, applying blood, and anointing with oil. These actions are reminiscent of Temple and pre-Temple sacrifices but quite distinct in their aesthetics. It has long been noted that even though animal sacrifice was an ancient practice in the Mediterranean basin, attitudes toward the practice shifted and changed over time. Explanations for this shift remain elusive. A general revulsion against animal sacrifice was in full swing by the first century B.C.E. and caused numerous traditional rituals to be reworked and reinterpreted.[37] This critique does not belong to any particular author or even a religious tradition, but shaped attitudes on a more widespread basis.

Describing this change in attitude demands some delicacy, since the emerging critique of sacrifices was often couched in ethicizing language. The rejection of animal sacrifice was presented as an improvement because killing animals, at least as part of cultic practices, was considered to be of questionable moral status. Ethicizing language was so pervasively employed for this development that it is difficult to see it as anything other than the moral evolution of religion (from magical animal sacrifices to purer internal sacrifices).

If we set aside the moralizing discourse, we can catch glimpses of changing ideas about what is appropriate or pleasing to divinities. Blood sacrifices seemed to offend against an emerging set of sensibilities according to which deity/deities were no longer thought to "eat." These shifting aesthetics were part of the impetus for Jews to turn to a heavenly cult and to the modified sacrifices discussed above.[38]

The standard view that prayer replaced sacrifice after the destruction of the Temple is an oversimplification that even rabbinic texts reject.[39] Modified sacrifices were part of the widespread Late Antique practice of rein-

37. See Wenschkewitz 1932 and Dahl 1941.

38. Against these shifting contours of thought, some individuals, such as the emperor Julian, supported animal sacrifices, including the plan to rebuild the Temple in Jerusalem. Given the tremendous shift away from animal sacrifice, these stances must have appeared quaint, if not downright backward, in other people's eyes. Because Julian frequently employed the term "theurgy" for his favorite rituals, his opponents may have seen this as evidence that "theurgy" referred to backward religious practices.

39. See the survey of rabbinic "histories" of sacrifices in Guttman 1967.

terpreting ancient animal sacrifice traditions.[40] The modified sacrifices appear to fulfill the gamut of purposes that animal sacrifices did, including purification and appeasing or inducing supernatural figures to fulfill specific requests. For example, Armand Delatte compiled a rich collection of modified sacrifices performed when collecting harvests and simple herb gatherings (1961:148–63). Prayers were said, and then offerings of honey, salt, grains, and even coins were made.

Central to these practices is the idea that sacrifice was directed not at the main deity but at lower-level figures, such as daimons and angels. This was the culmination of generations of thought about the meaning and function of ancient sacrifices. The notion that a deity might need or enjoy a sacrifice seemed outdated and aesthetically displeasing already with the writing of the final books of the Hebrew Scriptures.

One part of these reworkings of ancient sacrificial traditions was to argue that angels and daimons were nourished by the offerings. The Late Antique trope that daimons feed on sacrifices was "universal" (Chadwick 1965:146 n.1). Porphyry saw this as one of the reasons to reject animal sacrifice and adopt a vegetarian lifestyle. He claimed that daimons "rejoice in libations, and the savour of sacrifices, through which their pneumatic vehicle is fattened; for this vehicle lives through vapours and exhalations" (*On Abstinence* 2.42).[41]

Origen repeats many of the Late Antique clichés that daimons are "riveted" to "burnt-offering" and blood (*Against Celsus* 8.62) and "delight in frankincense and blood and the odors rising from burnt sacrifices" (4.32).[42] In fact, daimons desire sacrifices so much that they will try to steal the sacrifices designated for higher powers.[43] Diverse thinkers agree on this point. Origen shares it with his opponent Celsus as well as with

40. J. P. Brown (1979, 1980) comments on the rejection of sacrifice but does not say much about its reinterpretation. He does point to the important critique of sacrifice preserved in Porphyry *On Abstinence* 2.20. The alchemical practices, discussed in the next chapter, are another form of modified sacrifice.

41. See Philo *On the Decalogue* 74 and Oenomaus ap. Eusebius *Preparation for the Gospels* 5:21.

42. See *Exhortation to Martyrdom* 45. The specific reference to offerings here is from Homer *Iliad* 4.49, 9.50.

43. Origen also argues that evil powers were opposed to Jesus because he robbed them of their sacrifices (*Commentary on Matthew* 13.23).

many other groups, such as the Pythagoreans (3.28).[44] At one point, Origen discusses a figure called Aristeas who seemed uncomfortably similar to Jesus. According to Origen, Aristeas is in truth not a god but merely a daimon who obtained the reward of "drink-offering and burnt offering" (3.28).

Daimons are not the only supernatural beings who like sacrifices. Angels also feed off sacrifices, according to Origen. "Just as the demons, sitting by the altars of the Gentiles, used to feed on the steam of sacrifices, so also the angels, allured by the blood of the victims that Israel offered as symbols of spiritual things, and by the smoke of the incense, used to dwell near the altars and to be nourished on food of this sort" (*On First Principles* 1.8.1). This stunning statement of Origen's was almost certainly borrowed from Jewish reinterpretations of sacrifice traditions. The idea that sacrifices are "symbols of spiritual things" no doubt circulated in Jewish circles, which, as Yitzhak Baer pointed out, were among the early developers of such notions (1975). These reinterpretations were then projected back onto the founders of the sacrificial system. For example, in *Against Celsus* Origen explains that Moses knew about the connections between daimons and specific animals (4.92–93).

The *Book of Secrets* explicitly uses these ideas by claiming that it teaches the proper libations for the angels along with their names (1.9). The well-documented shift away from temple settings meant that these libations and other modified sacrifices could take place in a wide variety of locales.[45] In the *Book of Secrets* the locale for a specific rite is usually unspecified. In one instance the officiant is told to go to the spot where people have been killed (#8, 1.187), a standard locale for finding supernatural beings.[46] In the vast majority of cases the use of the sacrificial objects and the recitation of the formulas establish the site as a place where the officiants and supernatural helpers interact.

Some of the recipes employ objects in ways that do not seem to have

---

44. Origen cites a Pythagorean on this topic (*Against Celsus* 7.6) as well as Celsus (*Against Celsus* 8.60).

45. For a general discussion of the shift away from temples, see J. Z. Smith 1978: 172–89.

46. Supernatural spirits were thought to live near or in sources of water.

any connection with sacrificial traditions but that instead operate along the lines of analogies—that is, words are reinforced by actions that spell out the charge to the angels. The officiant, for example, smashes vessels to show exactly how the angel should smash an enemy (#2, 1.48).

Scholars have spilled more ink about the role of analogical thought and action than about any other topic related to ritual. James Frazer's famous laws of sympathy and contagion are both based on the notion that misguided analogies underlie "magic." His laws of contagion and like-effect-like imply that people mistakenly believe that sticking a pin in a doll will injure an enemy. As noted in the Introduction, however, this theory has been thoroughly critiqued in the past decades but is still implicated in most discussions of "magic."

Within the limits of this study, it seems most useful to point out that an important aspect of analogies is that they provide models of the desired results. The models are incorporated in the rites as formal representation of the goals—that is, actions can function iconically, just as words can. The formula against enemies and creditors, for example, asks the angels to "break his bones, to crush all his limbs, and to shatter his conceited power, as these pottery vessels are broken" (#2, 1.60). Both the words and the actions give an exact mapping of the desired end of the rite; they tell the angel exactly what the officiant wants to have happen to the enemy and then present a model of the completed action. Even without a verbal formula, the act of smashing vessels itself incorporates a specific instance of the action of "smashing" into the structure of the ritual.

In addition to iconic signification, in the context of the ritual, it is then possible to bring the desired ends into contact with a representation of the victim. The doll can be given the name of the victim or in some way associated with him or her. The verbal formula then directs the action specifically toward the intended victim, functioning as both an index and an icon. In term of its semiotics, the infamous "voodoo doll" represents iconically because it has a formal resemblance to the person to whom the rite is directed. Because the doll is associated with person *x*, it is an indexical sign, bringing the sign of a specific person into spatial-temporal contact with the harming supernatural forces.

These types of iconic actions appear throughout the recipes, both in this text and in most ritual texts from the Late Antique period. In all these cases, the use of icons is likely to arouse suspicions in the eyes of outsiders. Dionysius mockingly remarks that two plus two is the same as four—that is, he claims that the world is symbolic and not iconic. Without the specific understanding of the iconic status of elements of the rite, it looks from the outside as if something (doll/name) is simply mistaken as something else (victim/deity). In no case, however, is the act of smashing vessels understood in and of itself to effect the smashing of an enemy; that depends on the successful intervention of the forces that can do so (the angels, deity, and so on).

Four recipes lack oral recitations entirely but include written versions of angel names.[47] These recipes are for amulets to protect a soldier, a woman in childbirth, a person suffering from a headache or blindness, and a city. In the first three cases the person wears the amulet, in the fourth case a lamella is rolled up and placed under the heels of a statue in a special part of the city.

Jews commonly used amulets for protective purposes, and the practice was suspect only when the amulet was inscribed with the name of the wrong deity.[48] The amulets in the *Book of Secrets* include angel names, lacking the familiar biblical verses mentioned in rabbinic sources.[49] As noted above, the angel names are powerful not as tokens of divine speech, as biblical texts would be, but as iconic representations of the angels whose names contain the divine name "El."

Wearing a divine name on one's body both instantiates the divine presence and brings it in direct spatio-temporal contact with the wearer. This is true whether the name is written on an amulet that is then attached to the body, or whether the name is written directly on a limb.[50] Thus, in the terms of this study, amulets are icons that also function indexically, bringing the iconic power of the names directly into spatio-temporal contiguity with the wearer. In fact, this may be a good definition of an amulet, because what matters is that it directly represents the divine presence in a specific location (on a person, in a house).

47. No. 18, 2.110–12; #19, 2.123–25; #20, 2.134–38; #23, 2.182–85.
48. 2 Macc 12:40 and 1 Macc 5:67.
49. mShabbat 8:2, bShabbat 61b.
50. See Chapter 6.

The final point to make about the use of objects in "rites" is the notion of sympathy, common in Late Antiquity. Biblical notions of the selection of a certain animal for sacrifice do not play a great role in the modified sacrifices, which do not even always use the same animals. Instead, the rites assume notions of sympathy—that is, of a complex web of interconnections between all the elements employed in the rites and other dimensions of the cosmos. Once again it is the Neoplatonists who give us the most systematic explanations of these ideas. One of the clearest statements is the brief treatise *On the Hieratic Arts* composed by Proclus. This treatise both articulates the theoretical principles and gives a series of concrete examples of how these theoretical principles are manifested in the world.[51] The basic principle can be summed up as "Things on earth are full of heavenly gods; things in heaven are full of supercelestials; and each chain continues aboundingly up to its final members" (46–47).

This principle motivates diverse religious practices because each entity in the world relates to divinity in its proper manner—for example, the heliotrope flower follows the sun, and humans sing hymns. These specific techniques come from the gods themselves. The notion of sympathy also motivates the use of certain objects in rituals. The heavenly world can be found in earthly objects, so that they can represent specific cosmic forces on earth in ritual settings. Proclus mentions, for example, the divine connections of the cock, one of the animals used both in the *Book of Secrets* and in Greek ritual texts as well. Sympathy establishes a set of relationships between the seen and the unseen, opening up innumerable ways of using the material world to influence the immaterial. These unseen forces can both attract and repel, thus influencing the world in many ways that are not obvious to the human eye.

In Chapter 2 we discussed the ideology that divine speech is represented in the Torah in written form; the *Book of Secrets* intertwines the power of both written and spoken language. Amulets are placed on people's bodies, and formulas are spoken over them so that the goals are encoded in both spoken and written words. Each individual rite is a complex use of a number of iconic representations of supernatural powers, all of which are used indexically within each specific rite.

51. The Greek text is found in Bidez 1928, 6:139–51. An English translation is available in Copenhaver 1988:103–5.

THE SOCIAL CONTEXT OF THE *Book of Secrets*

If we turn briefly to the issue of social context, the relationship between the rituals in the *Book of Secrets* and rabbinic circles is a contested issue. The modern editor Margalioth characterized the ancient editor as distant from standard rabbinic circles due to his enthusiasm for talking to the dead and sacrificing to angels. Others have pointed to specific aspects of rabbinic thought that might allow someone to study a book such as the *Book of Secrets* for the purpose of understanding the practices—for example, Merchavya finds permission to study magic in various rabbinic citations.[52] Because Merchavya views the text as primarily theoretical, with recipes no human could hope to follow, he finds a close fit between the text and the particular rabbinic permission to study magic.

The text itself makes no claim in relation to rabbinic authority; no names of rabbis appear in it. The opening of the composition describes the text as "a book from the books of secrets" given by the angel Raziel[53] to Noah[54] before he went into the ark.[55] The claim to status as a heavenly book, a pre-Flood esoteric tradition revealed only to the few, was a common trope in Late Antiquity found throughout the apocrypha and pseudepigrapha.[56] It locates the text as a strand of tradition separate from other revelations, including, for example, the sacrificial laws in the Torah. The introduction specifically locates the text as a particularly old revelation with its own history and legitimacy.

While the tendency is to draw a sharp line between rabbinic practices and those in the lower six levels of the *Book of Secrets,* its rituals intersect with numerous anecdotes found scattered throughout the variegated corpus of rabbinic texts. The trope of rabbi as "holy man" has been explored for several decades;[57] Jacob Neusner sums it up neatly: "The rabbi knew the secret names of God and the secrets of the divine 'chariot'—the heav-

52. Merchavya points to such rulings as bSanhedrin 17a that the study of magic is permitted in order to understand it. He also points out that the later Hasidic Ashkenazim used these rulings to permit the study of magic for theoretical purposes (1966–67).

53. The angel name "Raziel" also appears on the seventh step in the second heaven.

54. In a variant, the text is given to Adam.

55. The text recounts a chain of transmission similar to mAvot 1:1.

56. See, for example, the reference to a Noahic book of healing in Jubilees 10:13.

57. See Green 1979; Neusner 1966–70, esp. 2:147–50, 3:102–26, and 4:347–70; and Levine 1975:86–106.

ens—and of creation. If extraordinarily pious, he might even see the face of the Shekinah . . . he could bring rain or cause drought. His blessing brought fertility, and his curses death. He was apt to be visited by angels and . . . he could see demons and talk with them, and could also communicate with the dead" (1969:10–11). It is easy to expand this list, pointing to stories where rabbis who were famed as healers[58] know the future and are capable of outwitting the angel of death.[59] Some claimed to have supernatural births, being not born of women,[60] and could control heat and fire.[61]

Even daimon sacrifices are mentioned in rabbinic texts, including casting bread into the sea for the daimon known as the Prince of the Sea (שר הים).[62] Lauterbach (1936) is probably correct that this practice was the basis for the popular Tashlich service, where individuals cast bread into a body of water for forgiveness of sins. The sea could intercede for people before God, as in the story of rewards given to a man who regularly sacrificed bread to the demon of the sea. Similarly, the obscure biblical ritual in which a goat is sent off into the wilderness to Azazel bearing the sins of Israel was understood by the rabbis to be a sacrifice to Satan.[63] Other texts mention sacrifices to demons such as pouring out oil and wine and scattering both parched grain and coins.[64]

At the same time, if some of the practices in the *Book of Secrets* contradict modern pictures of rabbinic practice, perhaps our picture of rabbinic Judaism remains too narrow. Saul Lieberman showed us the importance of using, for example, the attacks of Christians and Karaites as sources for evidence of lost rabbinic doctrines and practices (1939). Karaite denunciations of the rabbis emphasized their interest in angels, angel names, and the divine name, exactly as seen in the *Book*

---

58. R. Kahana cured R. Aha b. Jacob of jaundice (bShabbat 110b); R. Huna knows the remedy for tertian fever (bShabbat 67a).

59. bMoed Katan 28a and bMegilla 29a.

60. Samuel says of Rav Judah (bNidda 13a).

61. bTa'anit 21b.

62. See, for example, the reference to worshiping the Ruler of the Sea in bHullin 41b. The practice of throwing something into a lake is also denounced as a "Way of the Amorites."

63. *Pirkei de Rabbi Eliezer*, chap. 46, Lauterbach 1936:268–69.

64. tShabbat 7.16 (compare bBerakot 50b, Semahot 8). In addition to sacrifices, there were, of course, many other modes of relating to demons, including trying to drive them off or simply fooling them.

of Secrets.[65] Rabbinic practices included, for example, the use of incense[66]—the exact practice denounced in rabbinic sources when it is
done by women. Also denounced by the Karaites is the practice of putting blood on door posts on the 10th of Tevet and calling it "Korban,"
which is yet another modified sacrifice.[67] According to detractors, doing
so is acting too much in the image of the destroyed Temple. In all these
cases the gap between rabbinic practices and the rites in the *Book of
Secrets* narrows as we notice aspects of rabbinic practice that did not
attract much attention from previous generations of scholarship.

However, many of these practices, such as the daimon sacrifices, clearly
predated the rabbis and therefore may represent traditional practices over
which the rabbis had a difficult time gaining control.[68] The struggle to gain
control of supernatural forces seen in the *Book of Secrets* masks another
struggle, one that takes place entirely on the human plane. The rabbinic
corpus evinces conflicts between rabbis, both about practices they could
not control and with all sorts of competing figures who claimed access to
supernatural forces. Rabbis competed with necromancers, as in the story
of the necromancer who could predict an earthquake.[69] Dream interpreters beat rabbis at their own game, causing great distress to individual
rabbis by giving them bad dream interpretations that come true. Michael
Swartz raises the possibility that the scribes were another recognizable social group who had their own sources of legitimacy and power (1996).[70]

Women were another prime source of competition. Gentile women
have their own powers,[71] like the woman who cursed Rabbi Judah's ship
so that he had to put his clothes in water, thereby partially fulfilling and
thus averting the curse (bBaba Batra 153a). Even their own daughters can

65. See Nemoy 1930 and 1986.
66. See Lieberman 1939:76. This is to say nothing about the even stranger practice of ex-
changing gifts on Jesus' birthday mentioned in a sixth-century text.
67. See Lieberman 1939:76 and Mann 1931–35: 2:74.
68. Scholars tend to call these practices "popular," though the connotations of that term
in modern scholarship is in flux. It should not imply uneducated (as the rabbinic polemic
states) and so might best be referred to as extra-rabbinic.
69. bBerakot 59a, bTa'anit 21b.
70. The possibility that they had a role in making the ritual antidemon bowls so popular
in the Babylonian community is especially intriguing.
71. See bShabbat 81b, where a woman binds a boat so it will not move.

have powers that could threaten rabbis if out of their control, as in the case of the daughters of Rabbi Nahman who could stir a cauldron with their bare arms.[72]

Clearly the rabbis had no monopoly over the types of rituals the *Book of Secrets* presents as "rites." Honi the Circle-Drawer, the rabbinic competitor mentioned above, is ultimately "rabbinized" with the repeated retelling of his tale by rabbinic editors.[73] But Honi, and all the other figures mentioned, competed with rabbis in their roles as daimon specialists. The *Book of Secrets* may give us a window on one type of Jewish elite trying to keep successful methods from other individuals; these could include both rabbis opposed to specific ritual practices and nonrabbinic ritual specialists. These recipes are also being "rabbinized" in their presentation in the seven-heaven cosmology with the hymns on top, and by the association of this text with other *hekhalot* materials.

In the *Book of Secrets* we may see the shifting of the social setting for a series of rituals. The text makes secrets out of rituals that may at some earlier point have been under the control of other segments of society (not rabbis). The recipes are literally inserted into the upper realm, and the way up to the secrets is carefully guarded. Necromancers, rabbis' daughters, gentile women—what hope do they have of gaining access to these recipes now, even if these figures once engaged in the kinds of practices which the "secrets" represent?

This view gives us a new angle on the perennial question of the "rise of magic" in Late Antique society. The presumed culprit is usually "oriental" or even "Germanic" ideas that infect the Greco-Roman culture and doom its basic rationality. Contra this common view, Tamsyn Barton (1994) recently argued that there was less a "failure of nerve" than a shifting of the social setting for various types of practices. Specifically she argues that horoscopes gain a new prominence because the practice of astrology had gained influence in elite circles. The growing desire by those seeking to rule to prove their destiny as rulers through horoscopes brings the practice to the attention of modern scholars in a more dramatic manner.

Similarly, what we see in the *Book of Secrets* is in part the appropria-

72. bGittin 45a.
73. See Green 1979.

tion of rituals that may at other times have been practiced in diverse segments of society (women, men of deed, dream interpreters, and so on).
These rituals in turn attract the attention of modern scholars and are explained as the "rise of magic" or the contamination of Judaism by foreign
practices. One intriguing example of this is the imprecation of the sun.
This practice appears, on broader consideration, to have been much more
widespread in Jewish circles during the first centuries than once thought
(M. Smith, 1982). The types of evidence range from the staircase tower
described in the Temple Scroll (11Q19 col. 30), which has been connected
to sun worship among the Nabateans,[74] to references to similar practices
in Josephus (*Jewish Wars* 2.128)[75] and in various rabbinic texts.[76] This textual evidence correlates with the extensive archeological depictions of Helios, so prominent in synagogue mosaics. In the *Book of Secrets*,
imprecating the sun is neatly placed in the fourth heaven. Any individual
who does not have sufficient knowledge to gain access to the text (and the
fourth heaven) is not able to make use of this rite.

If the *Book of Secrets* had not been copied and thereby preserved, the
recipes would have been lost. This was the fate of many other rituals that
we know of only from hints found in the rich pseudepigraphic and apoc-
ryphal literature, as well as in the Qumran texts. The rabbis, to establish
themselves as the religious elite, had to be daimon experts par excellence
and as such displace others who claimed supernatural powers. The rise of
these figures is the shift away from a more widespread ability of individuals to intercede with supernatural powers to a focusing of that power in
the hands of only those with the special books, such as the *Book of Secrets*. This shift is a political shift as well and depends on the very this-
worldly ability of the elite to assert their control, not so much over
daimons as over their all-too-human rivals.

---

74. See Negev 1973.
75. Note the subsequent attempts to clean up Josephus' comments, M. Smith
1982:202*–203*.
76. See Lieberman's comments on bBerakot 9b (1974).

7

TRANSFORMATION BY DEED ALONE: THE CASE OF ALCHEMY

Whatever casts off the grossness
of the body becomes spirit.
—Zosimos, *On Virture* (Ber 3.6.1)

Among the marginalized rituals of Late Antiquity, the most neglected are the alchemical rites.[1] In contrast to the rituals discussed in previous chapters, these do not include any transformational language. There is no recitation of hymns or divine names and no descriptions of the heavenly world. Alchemical rites appear to have been silent rites in which attention was focused on elaborate devices used in heating metals.

With these rituals we have come to the "deeds-only" end of the spectrum, far from the rituals that consisted primarily of verbal formulas. The alchemical rites elaborate another model of reinterpreted sacrifices, distinct from the modified sacrifices found in the *Book of Secrets*. Once again the key to the rituals is the iconic status of the metals and, even more important, the iconic status of the changes made to them. These changes have a formal resemblance to the changes the world must undergo on its way to perfection.

There are, no doubt, many reasons for the neglect of these rituals. The technical aspects of the rituals have frightened away scholars. The texts are extremely difficult to comprehend, replete with unclear terminology and descriptions of obscure procedures. The only edition of the manuscripts, compiled by Berthelot over a century ago, is an idiosyncratic compilation;[2] all the manuscripts must ultimately be re-edited and new critical editions produced.[3]

---

1. For introductions to alchemy, see Riess 1893, 1:1338–55; Berthelot 1885; Festugière 1939 and 1950:217–82; and Forbes 1964:125.
2. Most of the manuscripts come from the tenth century on. The standard edition is

Ignored by scholars of religion, the texts have largely been claimed by historians of science and technology,[4] who have been responsible for what progress has been made in explaining the texts. The goal of these explanations is limited. The texts are of interest only to the extent that they prefigure certain aspects of modern science. In the eyes of historians of science, these texts are relegated to a few odd footnotes or held up as examples of good ideas gone wrong.[5] Yet the activities described in alchemical texts have scant relationship to the modern social practices and goals of science.[6]

The term "alchemy" is itself medieval; in late antiquity these rites were simply referred to as the "Sacred" or "Divine" Art or the "Great Work."[7] What then was the "Sacred Art"? The cliché of alchemy is that it constitutes the marriage of Greek philosophy and Egyptian technique.[8] In this equation, Greek philosophy means two or three citations from Aristotle or Plato about first causes and the primacy of matter; the Egyptian techniques are metalworking techniques. While it is possible to find precursors of alchemical ideas in classical Greek philosophical texts, this strategy for understanding alchemy generates a deceptively simple genealogy. This model also does little to explain how the Sacred Art articulated with Late Antique concerns.

Berthelot and Ruelle 1963 (*Ber*) (reprint of 1888). Berthelot prepared the Greek edition, which conflates several manuscripts. Ruelle edited some of the Greek and produced the French translation, which often varies from Berthelot's construal of such things as punctuation. The manuscripts are cataloged in Bidez et al. 1924:28.

3. New editions are currently under way, according to Halleux 1981, but only his one volume has appeared thus far.

4. The most useful discussions are in Taylor 1930, 1937, and 1949 and in Hopkins 1927 and 1934.

5. For example, Jensen writes that early chemists were "disappointed in their hopes" and so delivered the art into the hands of the masses, where it "deteriorated into the search for gold" (cited by Forbes 1948:19). Forbes himself writes: "The young chemistry had the typical rationalistic traits of the older Greek science. . . . Only relatively late in Antiquity can we speak of a degeneration when alchemical elements (in our sense) are introduced" (1948:19).

6. See the judicious comments by Tamsyn Barton (1994) about the distortion of ancient texts in modern histories of science.

7. For discussion of the term "alchemy," see Forbes 1964:126, and for numerous possible derivations, many of them fanciful, see Lindsay 1970:68–89.

8. See, for example, Festugière 1950. This view demands an earlier dating of the first alchemical texts because it is unlikely that Greek philosophy and Egyptian techniques came into contact only at the late dating (first century C.E.).

Instead of viewing early alchemy as the wedding of Greek thought and Oriental technique, alchemy is better understood as the harnessing of Late Antique τέχναι (arts/practical instructions) for religious goals. In the Late Antique period, "arts" were found in many areas of social practice, including rhetoric and medicine.[9] In the "Sacred Arts," religious thinkers attempted to co-opt, for their own quite distinct purposes, the prestige and success of the most up-to-date metal arts available.[10] The arts were put to work speeding up the inherent changes that the natural world (including humans) was believed to be undergoing. Two elements were required for the "sacred arts" to arise: first, a widespread perception that metalworking techniques could in fact succeed, and second, a well-developed theory of the transformable nature of the cosmos and human existence.

In approximately 290 C.E., an event occurred that Edward Gibbon (1946:285) and then Ernst Riess considered the first real event in the history of alchemy (1893:1341): Diocletian ordered the burning "of the ancient books of Chemia dealing with gold and silver" (περὶ χημείας ἀργύρου καὶ χρυσοῦ).[11] It is impossible to tell from the brief citation if these books were simply craft books or included the types of pursuits that interest us. Such distinctions may not have been of concern to Diocletian, who may not have cared whether gold was produced for monetary or salvific purposes. What this incident demonstrates is that some people, including people in high places, saw metalworking techniques as potentially successful and thus a threat. Techniques for producing gold had attracted attention in the highest circles and were considered effective—that is the first element necessary for alchemy.

The imagery we find in the writings of Zosimos (late third / early fourth

9. The arts offered practical instruction in medicine, rhetoric, architecture, and dream-interpretation, to name a few (Barton 1994:7).

10. "Stealing" metal-working techniques was similar to modern attempts to prove that penicillin, for example, is already prefigured in the Bible, thereby rubbing off on religion some of the enormous prestige science currently enjoys.

11. According to John of Antioch, Diocletian burned them so that men might not enrich themselves by this art and draw sources of wealth from it, which would enable them to revolt against the Romans (*Suda*, s.v. Diocletian). Diocletian also proscribed the "mathematici" (Codex Justinian 9.18.2). See Lippmann 1919:103.

century),[12] an active practitioner and codifier of alchemical treatises, res-
onates with Late Antique tropes. These tropes center on stories of the fall
of the first man into the body and his resulting subjection to Fate, and of
striving to transform nature and ascend beyond the body and Fate. In
Zosimos' version these tropes do not become standard "dualistic" thinking; instead, they retain a more positive attitude toward the natural world
because that world is in fact changing and changeable—the second element necessary for alchemy.

It is not clear when these elements, which form the basis of alchemy,
had emerged. Like the *hekhalot* texts, the alchemical texts are all based
on much later manuscripts and have numerous variants and problems.
We are heavily dependent on Zosimos' compilations for the early period
(pre–fourth century). Much of the writings of Zosimos are citations
from and discussions of Maria the Jewess and Pseudo-Democritus, both
of whom are difficult to date.[13] Pseudo-Democritus, is thought to have
flourished anywhere from the third century B.C.E. to the first century
C.E.[14] His only extant text is "Physical Things and Mysteries" (φυσικὰ
καὶ μυστικά),[15] although ancient writers associate other texts with his
name.[16]

12. Zosimos wrote before the Serapeum was destroyed in the 390s but cited Africanus,
who died in 232. For a concise introduction, see Jackson 1978:7. See Taylor 1937:88 on his
general importance. In general on Zosimos, see Plessner 1976, Riess 1893:1348, Forbes
1964:141, Lindsay 1970:323–57 (which must be used with care); and Hopkins 1934:69–77.
The writings of Zosimos are cited by the name of the treatise numbering in Berthelot's corpus, which is the same for the Greek and the French translation. This is a different mode of
citation than that followed by Patai, who cites the pagination from the French translation,
which is easy to confuse with the pagination of the Greek original and which he also occa-
sionally cites.

13. For citations of Maria, see Patai (1994:60–91). Unfortunately Patai worked with the
French translations of the texts and constructed his picture primarily from secondary discussions. This may be why there are numerous citation problems in his chapters on the
Greek alchemists. Patai supplies translations of many quotes from Maria but does not explain them in the context of Late Antique practices. While doing this would have led him off
the track from his emphasis on Jewish alchemists, it is necessary in order to make any sense
of Maria's turgid quotations.

14. Forbes conflates Pseudo-Democritus with an equally unknown author, "Bolos," who
also wrote a text called "Chircometa," and dates him to 200 B.C.E. (1964:138). Lindsay
takes a similar approach (1970: chaps. 5–6). See Halleux 1981:73.

15. *Ber* 2.1. This treatise is mentioned briefly in Chapter 3.

16. Pliny mentions a "Chircometa" (Artificial Substances) by Democritus, a term that appears in Zosimos, where it seems to mean metals produced by art (*NH* 24.160).

This particular text combines a mysterious revelation about the nature of nature with essentially practical methods of making gold-like and silver-like alloys familiar from contemporary metalworking techniques. It begins with formulas for dyeing cloth purple and then switches abruptly into a narrative about Pseudo-Democritus' search to learn how to "harmonize" nature. The search ends dramatically with the revelation of a phrase engraved on a pillar in a temple, "Nature rejoices in nature and nature conquers nature and nature masters nature," a cryptic saying that implies that natural processes can be used to change nature, to overcome nature. This is a very optimistic view, that the means for getting beyond the natural world are available in the natural world. Based on this premise, it is necessary to learn everything possible about the natural world because all answers are contained in it. If nature conquers nature, natural processes will ultimately lead to the cosmic changes sought by religious practitioners. This positive attitude toward the natural world is striking and is crucial to the development of the sacred arts.

Similar techniques also appear in the earliest extant papyri associated with alchemy, two papyri from a cache of four papyri dating from the mid-third century found in a tomb at Thebes.[17] The other two papyri, included as part of the *Greek Magical Papyri* (*PGM*), contain a now familiar hodgepodge of rites for healing, for sending dreams, and for causing love and hatred between people. One treatise, entitled the "Eighth Book of Moses," includes several versions of an initiation ritual (Leiden 12, *PGM* 13).[18] The two alchemical papyri appear on the surface very similar to handbooks for metalworkers (Leiden 10 and Stockholm).[19] Whoever compiled these recipes was not concerned about making jewelry, the usual task in metalworking, because none of these recipes appear to yield any practical results. While jewelry makers regularly succeed at their tasks, modern scholars speculate that these recipes were doomed to fail.[20]

17. French translation Berthelot 1938:28–77. The Greek with a French translation and introduction is available in Halleux 1981. On the Leiden papyrus, see Hopkins 1934:61–63. Other discussions include *Ber* 3–8; and Taylor 1930:111 and 1937:34–36.

18. Both papyri (Leiden 12 and 13) have numerous Jewish references, as noted by Patai 1994:56–57.

19. Halleux 1981:12.

20. See Pfister 1935.

In this rich find of papyri we see the adoption of metalworking techniques in new social settings and the severing of the techniques from simple (and obtainable) goals related to jewelry making. Creating the "Sacred Art" was in part establishing a new context for the techniques. The new context might be a collection of esoteric rituals; *Greek Magical Papyri* includes a recipe for tincture (ἴοσις) of gold right after a short formula for inducing a dream oracle (*PGM* 12.193–201). The fact that some alchemical rituals appear in the Greek ritual handbooks is no surprise, because, as argued below, these rituals are also forms of modified sacrifices. Within the spectrum of Late Antique rituals, the Sacred Art had close parallels to the modified sacrifices of Greek ritual handbooks.

THE RITUAL TECHNIQUES OF ALCHEMY

The basic goal of the alchemical procedures was to impart a series of color changes to the metals; blackening, whitening, yellowing, and, the most obscure, violet-making. Color was understood to be the spirit, the *pneuma*, of the metal,[21] indicating the inner nature of the metal to the outside world.[22] The change in the color of the metal is a sign that the metal is working its way up the cosmic ladder to a higher level.

Working with metals sets up a rich series of "standing for" relationships in the rites. The metals iconically represent the various components of the natural world because they are pieces of it, and thus share its form, and so forth. Each metal is iconic of a specific aspect of the natural world, as its color is a formal link with that level of the natural world. The change in coloration is also an iconic link with natural processes. Each change maps for the practitioner the process of transformation that the natural world undergoes.

In this thought system, metals stand at the center of a web of associations and analogies that permit their manipulation to have far-reaching religious significance. The metals represent the natural world, and changes in the metal are evidence of natural processes in action. The variety of

21. "All sublimed vapour is a spirit and such are the dyeing qualities" (Zosimos, "The Four Bodies," *Ber* 3.12.4).
22. See the short but important discussion by Forbes 1964:140.

metals permits the investigation of nature in its various aspects and concrete manifestations. Metals are "bodies," analogous to everything that has a body, including humans.

Metals are not static because the cosmic system is not static. As part of the unfolding natural world, they too change, or, as Arthur Hopkins describes it, they are "striving for perfection."[23] Regardless of its status in the natural world, its place in the hierarchy, every metal is on its way to being gold (Hopkins 1934:75). The structure of the cosmos includes perfection as a basic part of metals, all of which are gradually transforming to gold (Forbes 1964:132). The alchemist speeds up the process by adding a catalyst.

The basic change to which all these procedures is directed is transforming the metal from the state of having a body to not having one.[24] Maria the Jewess says, "If the corporeal is not rendered incorporeal, and the incorporeal corporeal, nothing that one awaits will take place" ("On the Body of Magnesium," *Ber* 3.28.8).The first stage is "blackening," a process that results in a primary substance considered to represent matter in its most basic state (an icon of pure substance). What this substance actually was is not clear. It could refer to an alloy of lead called "tetrasomy" ("four bodies") or an amalgam called "metal of magnesium," which could be broken down by being fused with sulfur.[25] This substance represented matter in its most embodied state and thus at the very bottom of the scale of nature; it was "unidentifiable by particular qualities."[26] Here individuality of matter was submerged, making a "body" that had no characteristics except that it was "fusible" (combinable with other matter) (Hopkins 1934:93). Fusibility was the only quality necessary to move the matter upward on the bodily scale toward greater liquidity.

23. Hopkins considers this an Aristotelian notion: "Accepting Aristotle's tendency toward perfection, the alchemists visualized the metals as striving to become as perfect as possible, to become white as silver or even yellow as gold so perfect that goodness and light should abound more and more and the 'sun metal' should illustrate the triumph of perfection over the primitive evil of the common 'earth metals'" (1934:37).

24. For Zosimos, becoming incorporeal is a means of overcoming fate ("On the Letter Omega," sec. 7).

25. See Forbes 1964:140–41. See also references to an alloy of copper and lead called "molybdocale" (*Ber* 3.28.2).

26. Hopkins (1934:92) notes Plato's concept of "first material," giving no specific quotation.

The alloy was then subjected to the second stage, "whitening." According to R. J. Forbes, this stage derives from general attempts to fake silver and its alloys (1964:14). The metal could be whitened by fusing to it tin or mercury or by adding a small bit of silver called a "ferment." Thus, it was possible to "whiten" a mass of metal by adding a small amount of "white." Hopkins notes that the addition of a small portion of silver "was supposed to gather to itself any silver already developed, so that when the black alloy was flooded with mercury or tin, the surface became glistening white and gave forth the appearance of silver."[27] While this alloy would be white only on the outside, the very fact that the inside was yellow would not have troubled an alchemist.[28]

The third step was yellowing. Fusing could be done with gold ferment this time, and the metal was yellowed with a substance referred to as "sulfur/divine water." The sulfur water had to be produced before it could be employed; it seems to have been made somehow from lead. Divine water was used because "it produces the transformation; by its application you will bring out what is hidden inside; it is called 'the dissolution of bodies'" (Pseudo-Democritus, "Synesius the Philosopher to Dioscorus," *Ber* 2.3.6). The resulting yellow substance could turn other substances yellow, again something that was not considered to be true of common gold.

The final and most obscure stage is ἴωσις, which appears to refer to giving the substance a purple or violet color, from the root *ios* (violet or rust).[29] This final step produced an "*ios* of gold" that was believed to be the essence with which pure gold could be produced. It represented iconically the highest form of physical existence. "It is the tincture forming in the interior [of the gold] which is the true tincture in violet, which has also been called the *ios* of gold" (Zosimos, "The Four Bodies," *Ber* 3.19.3).

If we have a vague understanding of these processes, we have less of a clear sense of the mixtures on which these procedures were performed. Basic to the esoteric nature of these texts is a secret language of metals.

27. Hopkins adds that arsenic and antimony were considered "mercury" (1934:95).

28. Because is it an alloy of copper, the alloy might be silver on the inside too, and thus look superior to regular silver (Hopkins 1934:96).

29. See Hopkins 1934:97–98. Taylor 1949:49–50 says that this stage could be either further tinting or simply cleaning of the metal or taking away the rust.

Metals as we know them cannot affect other metals; only when they are treated do they become agents of change. The ideology of "ferments" points to the special properties of the metals employed; none of them was the same as its mundane counterpart. "Each of them tints according to its own nature. Gold tints to gold; silver to silver" (Pelagus, "On the Divine and Sacred Art," *Ber* 4.1.8). This gold and silver is not what is commonly called gold and silver. Everything has its own nomenclature.[30] "'Our lead becomes black,' Maria explains, 'while common lead is black from the beginning'" (Zosimos, "About the Philosopher's Stone," *Ber* 3.29.1).

THE THEOLOGY OF ALCHEMICAL TRANSFORMATION

Most of the techniques are preserved without extensive theological introductions or commentaries. An important exception is Zosimos' treatise "On Virtue," where Zosimos articulates the analogy between working with metals and redeeming humans. In this treatise he presents a dream vision[31] in which he sees, as Jung described, "a kind of sacrificial act undertaken for the purpose of alchemical transformation" (Jung 1967:70). The Sacred Art is presented here with language familiar from sacrifice traditions. The alchemical rites do not include killing and eating animals, but the fire remains and the act of cooking is still there.

Alchemical authors relate their practices to ancient sacrificial traditions. In the Hebrew Temple, according to Zosimos' letter to Theosebeia, the sacrifices were prefigurations of the Sacred Art. The Hebrews tried to effect their own tinctures. He advises Theosebeia, "Without being asked, offer up sacrifices: . . . sacrifices such as those that were recommended by Membres when he addressed himself to Solomon, king of Jerusalem, and principally those which Solomon himself described according to his own wisdom."

The famous King Solomon, known internationally for his wisdom, is presented here as an alchemist. Because he built the Temple, he is most

---

30. One result of this is that Ruelle substitutes his notion of the "real" name of the substance in the French translation for the name in the Greek, such as "sulfur" for "lead."

31. The dream vision appears in the Berthelot edition in some disarray. For other translations and commentaries, see Taylor 1949:60–66 and Jung 1967, which includes an English translation by A. S. Glover of Jung's German translation.

closely associated with sacrifice traditions. A figure by the name of Membres does not appear in the biblical stories, and his identity is obscure.
Zosimos continues: "Operating in this manner you will obtain the proper,
authentic, and natural tincture. Make these things until you become perfect in your soul. But, when you recognize that you have arrived at perfection, then beware of [the intervention of] the natural elements of the
material: descending toward the Shepherd, and plunging into the krater
[bowl], you will thus re-ascend to your origin" ("The Final Reckoning,"
Ber 51.8).[32]

Familiar Late Antique religious goals—escaping the world below, returning to one's origin—are envisioned as the potential result of sacrifices
similar to those done by Solomon. The Hebrews in their Temple were
"perfecting" themselves by means of sacrifice, causing matter to ascend so
that it can escape the embodied state and thereby escape Fate as well.
Reascending to the highest heavens, a goal familiar from the extensive discussion of ascent in Chapter 5, is completed here by descending into the
krater, the bowl used in alchemical rites.

The theology of Zosimos includes complex notions of descent and ascent: alchemical secrets come from heaven, either via fallen angels, as
noted above, or via the ascent of a special individual who brings the secrets down.[33] So too the dream vision begins when Zosimos falls asleep
and sees seven steps leading up to an altar shaped like a krater.[34] The
krater is similar to the krater mentioned above in the letter from Zosimos
to his "sister" Theosebeia. Equipped with a krater, the altar is a flexible
implement in which a variety of types of "cooking" can take place, including, for example, both dipping and boiling.

In a vivid and stunning reinterpretation of sacrifice traditions, the entity sacrificed in the altar bowl is not an animal but the officiant.[35] The

32. This dense imagery is explicated somewhat in Zosimos' vision, which that is described here. Some of it remains unclear.

33. For Zosimos, Nikotheos appears to have been such an individual. See Jackson
1978:3.

34. Jung pointed to the use of a krater in the Hermetic tractate "Poimandres" as a parallel (1967:73).

35. Here the scale of sacrificial substitutes is worked backward and human replaces an
animal.

priest is both the sacrificer and what is sacrificed.[36] The meaning of the sacrifice is explicated in the dialogue between Zosimos and this officiant. Zosimos learns that by the "casting away of the grossness of the body" the priest who stands at the altar has become "in perfection as a spirit." The priest serves as the model of transformation; his body undergoes a series of changes until he reaches the highest goal. The priest's immersion, as Jung pointed out, leads to his transformation into a spiritual being (Jung 1967:73). At this point he is no longer has a body, but is instead spirit and thus perfect.

On a daily basis, Zosimos works with metals and not human bodies. By means of fire, the metal makes a dramatic progression upward to another type of existence, exactly as human bodies can. Each sacrifice is in effect a self-sacrifice in which "metal" bodies are harshly destroyed so that they can reach a new existence. Metallic bodies are cooked in a series of stages that led ultimately to gold, the most spiritual being. While Zosimos is working with these metals, a story about human bodies supplies the explanation for his practices. The Sacred Art, in this case, looks not toward only the special gold that is produced but toward the perfection of spirit and, most important, the spirit that is found in human bodies.

The process of change Zosimos sees in the vision is violent, as the priest "spewed forth all his own flesh." In the first stage he is burned, a process that is analogous to the "blackening" stage of working with metals. The priest is overpowered by a mysterious figure and dismembered: "And he drew off the skin of my head with the sword, which he wielded with strength, and mingled the bones with the pieces of flesh, and caused them to be burned upon the fire of the art, till I perceived by the transformation of the body that I had become spirit."

When Zosimos sees the altar again, the single figure has been replaced by a multitude of people who are undergoing the same treatment. The priest who sacrifices and is sacrificed has power over the other people who are being punished. The revelatory figure is now gray, and in the next section he becomes white, paralleling another step in the transformation of metal, the "whitening." The "white" man is engulfed in flames himself.

36. Noted by Jung 1967:70.

The procedure is completed when a god appears to him, marking the point of divine revelation. The god tells him that the head must be cut off and the flesh boiled. At the conclusion, Zosimos states that he understands "the art of the metals."

In Zosimos' vision, the processes are sped up before his very eyes so that he can see the entire sequence of cosmic processes in one dream. "Cooking" makes the stages appear in rapid order. What nature effects slowly by itself, the officiant in Zosimos' vision makes happen artificially fast. The intensified heat of the fire is one of the catalysts for the speed—that is, fire did not simply destroy, but instead transformed the natural world.

The entire procedure is then reviewed by Zosimos in a summary that stresses that the models for the transformation come from nature. "How does nature teach giving and receiving? . . . All things are woven together and all things are undone together" ("On Virtue" *Ber* 3.1.4). The rites were thought to mirror nature closely; the officiant is working with natural goals and natural processes. Someday all lead will naturally turn into gold; Zosimos' special talent is that he knows how to take control of the process and speed it up.

If the "utopian" vision sees a great gulf between matter and divinity, this vision evinces the opposite.[37] We learned from Pseudo-Democritus that all the answers can be found in nature. This is a very optimistic view; the means for getting beyond the natural world are obtainable from the natural world. Based on this premise, it is necessary to learn everything possible about the natural world because the answers are contained in it. If nature conquers nature, even without the interference of humans natural processes will ultimately lead to cosmic changes. The positive attitude toward the natural world is striking and is crucial to the theology of the Sacred Art.

Zosimos sees a continuum between the highest and the lowest elements in the cosmos. No radical break, no insurmountable gulf, separates the "grossness" of the body from the highest spirit, and nature itself in the form of fire can itself overcome that gap. The unseen forces of nature can be mapped in the changes of the metals, and all of this without any help

---

37. See Introduction, note 1.

from language at all. Like the ancient biblical sacrifices, which are presented at least in some texts as being carried out in silence, the alchemical rites included no names, prayers, or sounds. At the same time, they could bring about even more dramatic transformations than the adjurations. The forces that brought about the transformations were mysterious, because they were largely unseen by the average human being. Zosimos and his fellow practitioners considered them divine.

CONCLUDING NOTE

This study points to the tremendous diversity of religious ideas at the turn of the millennium. The Late Antique world presented a plethora of ways for individuals to interact with, direct, beseech, and thwart gods, angels, and daimons. Centuries-old rituals (sacrifice) were reinterpreted, and new ones (ascent) were created. Sometimes these rituals were based on traditional notions of the alignment between heaven and earth with sacrifices as the basic model for intercession, purification, and thanksgiving. Ancient notions of sacrifice were reworked based on contemporary ideas of the role of the deity and of demons. These reworkings depended on notions of sympathy and antipathy. The practitioners of these rituals remained fundamentally optimistic in that they thought the gap between earth and heaven could be overcome using tradition ideas of communication and interaction. Other theological models competed with this view, including many that pointed to an unbridgeable gap between the corrupt earthly sphere and the divine immortal world of the highest heavens. In these cases, rituals had to be as "otherworldly" as possible, and thus cut off from matter in all its forms.

Speculation and action across the theological spectrum were based on Late Antique notions of efficacy. These may appear obscure to both ancients and moderns, who have their own, often unexamined notions of how the world works. Lurking behind the ritual texts are issues of power, and in this case human power. Not everyone had access to the texts, nor was everyone permitted to engage in the practices.

Religious practitioners in the first centuries C.E. could show their power by their knowledge of cosmic secrets, divine names, and other esoteric traditions. A friend of the highest-level supernatural powers, he (and in rare cases she) could put into play divine power based on socially conceived notions of efficacy. To have the religious experience of ascent through the heavens is to be permanently changed; to produce gold is to thoroughly know and control the natural forces. In Late Antiquity, a human form could conceal a vast array of powers, and the esoteric rituals may reveal a human to be a supernatural expert walking around in a human body.

Particular attention was given in Late Antiquity to exegesis of the name of the deity. We witness a tremendous exchange of ideas about divine names across religious traditions. Current scholarly understanding of this exegesis tends to isolate these ideas as distinct from, and inferior to, other modes of religious expression. This is not without irony, because the divine name was considered especially holy. God's name was equated with his creative power, and, as in the Aramaic Targums, the "content" of that name was the very act of creative speaking itself. For these Jewish writers, the divine name was not only the metaphysical origin of all language but also the source of efficacy in ritual language even at the level of the sounds of the name.

All these ideas are predicated on the function of the divine name as a particular type of sign, specifically its function as an icon. It is impossible to understand this function of the name—and to compare it with other possible ways in which words and signs can function—without the very specific semiotic vocabulary of icon, index, and symbol. The larger iconic structure of ritual texts also turned out to be crucial, not only in the ascent hymns but also in the mirroring of the cosmic levels in the *Book of Secrets*.

For the Hebrew exegetes, the deity spoke Hebrew, permitting a basic analogy between divine speech and human speech. This is important for Origen because it permits a direct link between the levels of meaning in Hebrew and the divine world, between the process by which the world was created and the potentials of human language. For other Christians this analogy was less powerful. Almost metaphorically, Jews become "literalists" no matter how they read scriptural texts because they read Hebrew (the letter) while the Christians interpret the Greek (the spirit).

For Dionysius the Aeropagite, names did not carry any inherent power based on their sounds, but they were still crucial guides to the divine world and capable of transforming the symbols of bread and wine, and humans as well. For everyone, language merited careful thought and analysis because the deity chose it to create the world and convey his revelation. Both Name and Word are mysterious in their ability to manifest divine reality and power to humans on earth. Many of these ideas were no doubt influenced by the general culture (Greco-Roman concepts of names and numbers), because they are not simple biblical concepts. These ideas were developed by the Jews and then in turn borrowed by other groups based on stereotypes of who had the oldest wisdom.

All these effective units—names, letters, and sounds—can be harnessed for diverse ritual ends. Human practitioners can transcend their earthly existence and enter the divine realm by means of special use of language. Talking like angels assimilates a human individual into the group of heavenly worshipers. Ascent is the model on which so many Late Antique ritual texts are built because it articulates with the contemporary vision of a multilayered and hierarchical cosmos. This cosmology belonged to no specific religious tradition, and neither did notions of ascent. The ritual model of ascent was applied to numerous goals, from the mundane purpose of thwarting enemies to the seemingly heretical goal of transforming a human into a cosmic being.

The sum-total of techniques in the ascent are familiar: the appropriation of heavenly cultic activities by humans, such as reciting praises, combines with wearing amulets and with the special power of the divine names. No techniques are unique to *Hekhalot Rabbati,* or to ascent for that matter. Instead, the key to ascent is using these techniques within the structure of ascent.

The proper words were also key to summoning angels in the *Book of Secrets.* With angelic aid, practitioners are able to thwart or accomplish a wide range of goals; this is striking because the rites represent a microcosm of human wishes, from the petty and even vain to the dramatic and transformative. Employing angels demands knowledge not only of cosmic secrets but also of the workings of this-worldly legal language. The elaboration of the ritual comes in the constant interplay between getting the angel to go to work, supplying exotic ingredients, and remembering the formulas. The focus of the text is on the ability of the officiant to insinuate himself higher and higher into the cosmic order and finally arrive at a level where he does not have to manipulate lower-level supernatural

forces but instead needs only declare the deity blessed. The perceived efficacy of the verbal formulas is clearer to the user than, for example, the
manipulation of objects, because an adjuration transparently appears to
the reciter to "do something." Because the efficacy of swearing is more
self-evident to users than some of the manipulations of objects, the adjurations are more adaptable as effective ritual devices. They may continue
to be copied while many of the actions will fall out of a text. For example,
in the collection of recipes known as "The Sword of Moses," some sections consist entirely of verbal adjurations that have lost their other components (Gaster 1971:288–337).

In the Late Antique context, the alchemical investigations into nature
sought to uncover the most secret layers of existence and thereby permit
the practitioner to step in and control nature. Instead of reciting names or
using heavenly liturgy, the participant strives to uncover the processes that
shape the entire cosmos. Once these processes are understood at the level
of the natural world, and in particular in metals, anything, even humans,
can be transformed into a higher existence. Again, the key to the transformative aspects of the rites is the complex iconic "standing for's" that
the rites entail. The metals are icons of the basic structure of the cosmos
in a very literal way, being actual bits of cosmic elements. The base metal
produced in the first part of the alchemical procedures has the exact form
(and even more) of the lowest end of the cosmos, and even more so because it is more base than any naturally occurring metal. The transformations are also iconic because they map for us, in a fast and visible way, the
transformations of the natural world.

As for the structure of these rituals, the mode of operation is highly
technical and based mainly on the construction of elaborate ritual devices
for manipulating metals. Ritual technique focuses on the sheer complexity of these devices, and not at all on the correct formulas or blessings. No
ritual formulas are recited at all, which is in striking contrast to the heavily word-based ascent rituals.

The alchemical circles, gathered around their flames, worked with
complex concoctions that are now lost to us. These rites were predicated
on the view that no unbridgeable gap exists between the highest and lowest parts of the cosmos. However much it might look like "lead," the

world was on its way to becoming "gold," and it was within one's grasp to uncover and effect this process. The endeavors must have seemed wildly optimistic to many of the alchemists' peers, who believed that the gap between the world of nature and the world of the mind was too great to overcome.

Contrast these actions with the rabbinic anecdote about the two rabbis who studied a Book of Creation and were able to create a cow. Their investigation involves no search for a lion cub, no collecting of water from seven streams in pure vessels, no collecting of metals and odd utensils. This esoteric "praxis" was thoroughly "spiritualized" and included only manipulation of language. Ritual elaboration in this system comes in the endless spinning of new permutations of the central ritual word—the name of the deity—and in endless playing with the letters.

For all these rituals we depend on textual traditions that are fraught with problems. Fortunately, the rituals were conceptualized in dialogue with discussions of efficacy found in texts that are somewhat easier to date. The philosophical grounding of rituals point to two stages. The first is a nascent stage in the first centuries B.C.E. through the first centuries C.E., when ideas that would be crucial to later ritual were just developing (ideologies of the name, the transformational potential of nature, the possibility of a human ascending). By the third and fourth centuries the ritual techniques analyzed here had undergone substantial development; we find movements to edit and collect sets of ritual techniques, both of the alchemical type and of the types found in the *Book of Secrets*. By the third and fourth centuries, we also see evidence of hostile debate and attack, as those who want to be thought of as normative and "traditional" establish their positions by rejecting some of these religious traditions (for example, rabbinic controversies over ascent).

Ancient thinkers were aware of the contrasting modes of approaching divinity. Damasicius grouped Plotinus and Porphyry as "philosophers" against Iamblichus, Syrianus, and Proclus as "hieratics" (*Commentary on the Phaedo*). Among those who employed rituals, there were divergent ideas about how to construct the rituals—whether "words only" rites were superior to other types of ritual actions.

Late Antique debates about the aesthetics of ritual may in turn mask the radical claims of many of the practitioners. Some Jewish, Christian, and Greco-Roman ancient writers were unified on one point: the lofty goals of their rituals. Socrates is reported to have said that his aim was to "become godlike" (*Theaetetus* 176B); whatever he might have meant, it was his follower the Chaldaean Platonist Julian who prayed that his son would have the soul of an archangel and who saw himself as one in a chain of divine beings placed temporarily in a human body.

With the proper intention, the very best rituals can have, for Iamblichus, the same results as Plotinus' investigations: ἕνωσις (union). Divination, for Iamblichus, "unites us with the divine" (*On the Mysteries* 10.4; 2.289.3–6). The best rituals, theurgy, played their part by purifying and saving the soul (1.12; 41.13 and 10.7; 293.5–8). His ultimate ritual goal was "to put on the form of the god" (4.2; 184.8) and exchange his life for a new divine existence (3.4; 109, 14–15). For Dionysius, rituals can both transform the bread and wine and also deify the officiant.

If these notions of ritual efficacy are not relegated to the margins of religious expression as either "magic" or "mysticism," some stereotypes of Late Antique religious expressions fade. For practitioners all across the spectrum, rituals were a path of transformation from earthly to heavenly existence. For those who believed in the existence of supernatural powers, all the rituals we have examined offered both the deadliest and the most holy potential.

1. See Protrepticus chap. 8, p. 48, 9–21.

SELECT BIBLIOGRAPHY

PRIMARY SOURCES

(Texts cited according to the Loeb editions are not included in this list.)

Albinus. *Eisagogue [Introduction to Platonic Thought]*. In *Plato*, vol. VI, pp. 147–51. Ed. Hermann. Teubner: Leipzig, 1936.

Artemidorus. *Oneirocritica [The Interpretation of Dreams]*. Translation and commentary by Robert J. White. Park Ridge, N.J.: Noyes Press, 1975.

Censorinus. *De die natali [Concerning the Day of Birth]*. Ed. N. Sallman. Teubner: Leipzig, 1983.

Book of Secrets. Sepher ha-Razim: The Book of the Mysteries. Trans. Michael A. Morgan. Chico, Calif.: Scholars Press, 1983.

The Chaldean Oracles. Text, translation and commentary by Ruth Majercik. Leiden: Brill, 1989

Corpus Hermeticum. Trans. A. J. Festugière. Ed. A. D. Nock Paris: Les Belles Lettres, 1954–60.

———. English translation: *Hermetica*. Trans. Brian Copenhaver. Cambridge: Cambridge University Press, 1992.

Damascius, *Commentary on the Phaedo* in *Greek Commentaries on Plato's Phaedo* vol. 2. Ed. L. G. Westerink. Amsterdam and New York: North-Holland, 1976

Dionysius the Areopagite. *Pseudo-Dionysius: The Complete Works*. Trans. Colm Luibheid. New York: Paulist Press, 1987.

Greek Magical Papyri in Translation. Ed. Hans Dieter Betz. Chicago: University of Chicago Press, 1986.

Iamblichus. *Iamblichus: On the Pythagorean Life*. Translated with notes and introduction by Gillian Clark. Liverpool: Liverpool University Press, 1989.

———. *Jamblique: Les Mystères d'Egypte [On The Mysteries]*. Trans. and ed. E. des Places. Paris: Les Belles Lettres, 1966.

———. *Theologumena Arithmeticae [Theology of Mathematics]*. Ed. V. deFalco, 1922. Edited with additions and corrections by U. Klein. Stuttgart: Teubner, 1975

———. *In Platonis Dialogos Commentariorum Fragmenta [Commentary on the Timaeus]*. Trans. and ed. John Dillon. Leiden: E. J. Brill, 1973.

Masseket Hekhalot. In *Bet Ha-Midrasch* vol. 4. Ed. Adolph Jellenik. Jerusalem: Wahrmann Books, 1967.

Merkaba Rabba. Synopse zur Hekhalot-Literatur. Ed. Peter Schäfer, Margarete Schlüter, Hans-Georg von Mutius. Tübingen: Mohr, 1981.

——. *The Shi'ur qomah: texts and recensions.* Ed. Martin Samuel Cohen. Tübingen: Mohr 1985.

Midrash Konen, In Jellenik 1967, see *Masseket Hekhalot.*

Musici scriptores graeci [Greek Writers on Music]. Ed. Karl von Jan. Leipzig: Teubner, 1895.

Proclus. *Elements of Theology.* Ed. E. R. Dodds. Oxford: Oxford University Press, 1963.

——. *Commentary on the First Alcibiades of Plato.* Ed. L. G. Westerink. Amsterdam: North-Holland, 1954. English translation by W. O'Neill. The Hague: Martinus Nijhoff, 1965.

——. *In Platonis Rem Publicam Commentarii [Commentary on the Republic].* Ed. W. Kroll. Leipzig: Teubner 1899–1901.

——. *In Platonis Timaeum Commentaria [Commentary on the Timeaus].* Ed. E. Diehl. Leipzig: Teubner, 1903–6.

——. *In Platonis Cratylum Commentaria [Commentary on the Cratylus].* Ed G. Pasquali. Leipzig: Teubner, 1908.

——. *Théologie platonicienne [Platonic Theology].* Trans. and ed. H. D. Saffrey and L. G. Westerink. Paris: Les Belles Lettres, 1968–87.

Pseudo-Dionysius. *See* Dionysius the Areopagite.

Sepher ha-Razim. See *Book of Secrets.*

Targum Neofiti. Neophyti 1. Targum Palestinense Ms. de la Biblioteca Vaticana. Ed. A. Díez Macho. Madrid: Consejo Superior de Investigaciones Científicas, 1968–79.

Targum Pseudo-Jonathan. Targum Pseudo-Jonathan of the Pentateuch. Ed. E. G. Clarke, W. E. Aufrecht, et al. Hoboken, N.J.: Ktav, 1984.

Theodosius Alexandrinus. *See* Iamblichus.

Zosimos. "On the Letter Omega." *See* Jackson 1978.

SECONDARY SOURCES

Albeck, Hanokh. 1952. *Shishah sidrei mishnah.* Tel Aviv: Mosad Bialik.

Alexander, P. S. 1983a. "Review of Peter Schäfer's *Synopse zur Hekhalot-Literatur.*" *Journal of Jewish Studies* 34:102–6.

——. 1983b. "Third Enoch." Pages 223–315 in *Old Testament Apocrypha and Pseudepigrapha,* vol. 34, ed. James Charlesworth. Garden City, N.Y.: Doubleday.

——. 1986. "Incantations and Books of Magic." Pages 342–79 in *The History of the Jewish People in the Time of Jesus Christ,* ed. G. Vermes, F. Millar, and M. Goodman. Third edition. Edinburgh: Clark.

——. 1987a. "Prayer in the Heikhalot Literature." Pages 43–64 in *Priere, mystique et judaisme: Colloque de Strasbourg, 10–12 septembre 1984,* ed. Roland Goetschel. Travaux du Centre d'histoire des religions de Strasbourg 2. Paris: Presses Universitaires de France.

——. 1987b. "Third Enoch and the Talmud." *Journal for the Study of Judaism* 18:40–68.

——. 1990. "Jewish Aramaic Translations of Hebrew Scriptures." Pages 217–54 in *Mikra: Text, Translation, Reading, and Interpretation of the Hebrew Bible in Ancient*

Judaism and Early Christianity, ed. M. J. Mulder and Harry Sysling. Minneapolis, Minn.: Fortress Press.

———. 1992. "Targum, Targumim." Pages 320–31 in *The Anchor Bible Dictionary,* vol. 6, ed. David Noel Freedman. New York: Doubleday.

Alon, G. 1950. "In the Name." *Tarbits* 21:30–39. Hebrew.

Altmann, Alexander. 1946. "Sacred Hymns in Hekhaloth Literature." *Melilah* 2:1–24.

Aptowitzer, Victor. 1930–31. "The Heavenly Temple in the Aggadah." *Tarbits* 2:257–87. Hebrew.

Asad, Talal. 1993. *Genealogies of Religion: Discipline and Reasons of Power in Christianity and Islam.* Baltimore: Johns Hopkins University Press.

Athanassiadi, P. 1993. "Dreams, Theurgy, and Freelance Divination: The Testimony of Iamblichus." *Journal of Roman Studies* 83:115–30.

Austin, J. L. 1962. *How to Do Things with Words.* Oxford: Clarendon Press.

Bacher, W. 1901. "Shem Ha-Meforash." Pages 262–64 in *Jewish Encyclopedia,* vol. 11, ed. I. Singer. New York: Funk & Wagnalls.

Baer, Yitzhak. 1975. "The Service of Sacrifice in Second Temple Times." *Zion* 40:95–153.

Bardy, Gustave. 1937. "Les traditions juive dans l'oeuvre d'Origene." *Revue Biblique* 34:220–40.

Bar-Ilan, Meir. 1989. "Magical Seals Written on Bodies." *Tarbits* 40:37–50. Hebrew.

Barton, Tamsyn. 1994. *Ancient Astrology.* New York: Routledge.

Baumgarten, J. 1986. "The Book of Elkesai and Merkabah Mysticism." *Journal for the Study of Judaism* 17:212–23.

———. 1988. "The Qumran Shirot and Rabbinic Merkabah Traditions." *Revue de Qumran* 13:199–213.

Berthelot, Marcellin. 1885. *Les origines de l'alchimie.* Paris: G. Steinheil.

———. 1938. *Introduction à l'étude de la chimie des anciens et du moyen-âge.* Paris: Librarie des Sciences et des Arts.

Berthelot, Marcellin, and C. Ruelle. 1963. *Collection des anciens alchimistes grecs.* London: Holland Press. Reprint of 1888.

Betz, Hans Dieter. 1986. *The Greek Magical Papyri in Translation.* Chicago: University of Chicago Press.

Bickerman, E. J. 1929. "Die Römische Kaiserapotheose." *Archiv für Religionswissenschaft* 27:1–31.

———. 1980. *Chronology of the Ancient World.* London: Thames & Hudson.

Bidez, Joseph. 1964. *Vie de Porphyre, le philosophe neo-platonicien: Avec les fragments des traites Peri agalmaton et De regressu animae.* Hildesheim: G. Olm. Reprint of 1913.

———. 1965. *La vie de l'empereur Julien.* Paris: Les Belles Lettres. Reprint of 1930.

Bidez, Joseph, et al. 1924–28. *Catalogue des manuscrits alchimiques grecs.* Bruxelles: M. Lamertin.

Bietenhard, Hans. 1974. *Caesarea, Origenes und die Juden.* Stuttgart: W. Kohlhammer.

Blau, Ludwig. 1914. *Das altjüdische Zauberwesen.* Berlin: L. Lamm.

Bloch, P. 1893. "Die *ywrdy mrkbh,* die Mystiker der Gaonenzeit und ihr Einfluss auf der

Liturgie." *Monatschrift für Geschicht und Wissenschaft des Judentums* 37:18–25, 69–74, 57–266, 305–311.

Blowers, Paul. 1988. "Origen, the Rabbis, and the Bible: Toward a Picture of Judaism and Christianity in Third-Century Caesarea." Pages 98–116 in *Origen of Alexandria: His World and His Legacy,* ed. C. Kannengiesser and W. L. Petersen. South Bend, Ind.: University of Notre Dame Press.

Böhlig, A., and F. Wisse. 1975. *Nag Hammadi Codices III,2 and IV,2: The Gospel of the Egyptians.* Leiden: Brill.

Bokser, Baruch. 1985. "Wonder-Working and the Rabbinic Tradition: The Case of Hanina ben Dosa." *Journal for the Study of Judaism* 16:42–92.

Boll, Franz. 1903. *Sphaera: Neue griechische Texte und untersuchungen zur geschichte der Sternbilder.* Leipzig: Teubner.

Bousset, Wilhelm. 1901. "Die Himmelreise der Seele." *Archiv für Religionwissenschaft* 4:136–69, 229–73.

———. 1923. *Apophthegmata.* Aalem: Scientia.

Boyer, Louis. 1980. "Mysticism: An Essay on the History of the Word." Pages 42–55 in *Understanding Mysticism,* ed. Richard Woods. New York: Doubleday.

Brandt, Edward. 1927. *Untersuchungen zum Romischen Kochbuche: Versuch einer Losung der Apicius-Frage.* Philologus Supplementband 19, Heft 3. Leipzig: Dieterich.

Brightman, F. E. 1965 (1896). *Liturgies, Eastern and Western, Being the Texts, Original or Translated, of the Principal Liturgies of the Church.* Oxford: Clarendon Press.

Brown, J. P. 1979. "The Sacrificial Cult and Its Critique in Greek and Hebrew, Part 1." *Journal of Semitic Studies* 24:159–73.

———. 1980. "The Sacrificial Cult and Its Critique in Greek and Hebrew, Part 2." *Journal of Semitic Studies* 25:1–21.

Carmi, Ted. 1981. *The Penguin Book of Hebrew Verse.* New York: Viking Press.

Chadwick, Henry, ed. and trans. 1965. *Origen: Contra Celsum.* Cambridge: Cambridge University Press.

Charlesworth, James H. 1983. *The Old Testament Pseudepigrapha,* vol. 1. Garden City, N.Y.: Doubleday.

Cohen, Martin Samuel. 1983. *The Shi'ur qomah: Liturgy and Theurgy in Pre-Kabbalistic Jewish Mysticism.* Lanham, Md.: University Press of America.

———. 1985. *The Shi'ur qomah: Texts and Recensions.* Texte und Studien zum antiken Judentum 9. Tübingen: Mohr.

Cohon, S. 1951. "The Name of God: A Study in Rabbinic Theology." *Hebrew Union College Annual* 26:579–604.

Collins, John. 1985. "Artapanus." Pages 889–903 in *The Old Testament Pseudepigrapha,* ed. James Charlesworth. Garden City, N.Y.: Doubleday.

Copenhaver, Brian. 1988. "Hermes Trismegistus, Proclus, and the Question of a Philosophy of Magic in the Renaissance." Pages 79–110 in *Hermeticism and the Renaissance,* ed. Ingrid Merkah and Allen Debus. Washington, D.C.: Folger.

Dahl, Nils. 1941. *Das Volk Gottes: Eine Untersuchung zum Kirchenbewusstsein des Urchristentums.* Darmstadt: Wissenschaftliche Buchgesellschaft.

Dan, Joseph. 1967–68. "Review of *The Book of Secrets.*" *Tarbits* 37:208–214. Hebrew.

———. 1979. "The Concept of Knowledge in the Shiur Komah." Pages 67–73 in *Studies in Jewish Religious and Intellectual History: Presented to Alexander Altmann on the Occasion of His Seventieth Birthday*, ed. Alexander Altmann, Siegfried Stein, and Raphael Loewe. Tuscaloosa: University of Alabama Press.

Davila, James. 1993. "Prolegomena to a Critical Edition of the Hekhalot Rabbati." *Journal of Jewish Studies* 44:208–25.

Deissmann, G. Adolf. 1895. *Bibelstudien*. Marburg: N. G. Elwert.

Delatte, Armand. 1961. "Herbarius: Recherches sur le cérémonial usité chez les anciens pour la cueilette des simples et des plantes magiques." *Memoires Academie Royale de Belgique*, vol. 54.

Dieterich, A. 1891. *Abraxas: Studien zur Religionsgeschichte*. Leipzig: Teubner.

Diez Macho, Alejandro. 1960. "The Recently Discovered Palestinian Targum." *Vetus Testamentum Supplement* 7:222–45.

———. 1979. *Neophyti 1, Targum Palestinense ms. de la Biblioteca Vaticana*. Madrid: Consejo Superior de Investigaciones Cientificas.

Dillon, John. 1985. "The Magical Power of Names." *Origeniana Tertia: The Third International Colloquium for Origen Studies, University of Manchester September 7th–11th, 1981*, ed. R. P. C. Hanson and Henri Crouzel. Rome: Edizioni dell'Ateneo.

———. 1996. "Oaths." Pages 1056–57 in *The Oxford Classical Dictionary*, ed. Simon Hornblower and Anthony Spawforth. New York: Oxford University Press.

Dodds, E. R. 1947. "Theurgy and Its Relationship to Neoplatonism." *Journal of Roman Studies* 37:55–69.

———. 1961. "New Light on the 'Chaldaean Oracles.'" *Harvard Theological Review* 54:263–73.

Dodds, E. R., ed. and trans. 1963. *Proclus' The Elements of Theology*. Second edition. Oxford: Clarendon Press.

Dornseiff, Franz. 1922. *Das Alphabet in Mystik und Magie*. Leipzig. Berlin: B. G. Teubner.

Duranti, Alessandro. 1992. "Language in Context and Language as Context: The Samoan Respect Vocabulary." Pages 77–100 in *Rethinking Context: Language as an Interactive Phenomenon*, ed. Alessandro Duranti and Charles Goodwin. Cambridge: Cambridge University Press.

Elior, Rachel. 1990. "Merkabah Mysticism: A Critical Review." *Numen* 37:233–47.

———. 1993–94. "Mysticism, Magic, and Angelology: The Perception of Angels in Hekhalot Literature." *Jewish Studies Quarterly* 1:3–53.

———. 1999. "The Merkavah Tradition and the Emergence of Jewish Mysticism." Pages 101–58 in *Sino-Judaica: Jews and Chinese in Historical Dialogue*, ed. Aharon Oppenheimer. Tel Aviv: Tel Aviv University.

Ervin-Tripp, Susan. 1976. "Is Sybil There? The Structure of American English Directives." *Language in Society* 5:25–66.

Faraone, Christopher. 1991. "The Agonistic Context of Early Greek Binding Spells." Pages 3–32 in *Magika Hiera: Ancient Greek Magic and Religion*, ed. C. Faraone and D. Obbink. New York: Oxford University Press.

Ferwerda, R. 1982. "Plotinus on Sounds: An Interpretation of Plotinus' *Enneads* V.5.519–27." *Dionysius* 6:43–57.

Festugière, A. J. 1939. "Alchymica." *L'Antiquité Classique* 8:71–95.

———. 1950. *La Révélation d'Hermes Trismégiste*, vol. 1. Paris: Gabalda Press.

———. 1967. *Proclus. Commentaire sur le Timée*. Paris: J. Vrin.

———. 1971. *Etudes de philosophie grecque*. Paris: J. Vrin.

Fitzer, G. 1971. "Sphragis." Pages 7:939–53 in *Theological Dictionary of the New Testament*, ed. Gerhard Kittel, Geoffrey William Bromiley, and Gerhard Friedrich. Grand Rapids, Mich.: Eerdmans.

Flesher, Paul. 1995. "The Targumim." Pages 40–63 in *Judaism in Late Antiquity, Part 1: The Literary and Archaeological Sources*. Leiden: Brill.

Forbes, R. J. 1948. *Short History of the Art of Distillation*. Leiden: Brill.

———. 1964. "The Origin of Alchemy." Pages 125–48 in *Studies in Ancient Technology*, vol. 1, ed. R. J. Forbes. Leiden: Brill.

Fossum, Jarl E. 1985. *The Name of God and the Angel of the Lord: Samaritan and Jewish Concepts of Intermediation and the Origin of Gnosticism*. Tübingen: Mohr.

Fowden, Garth. 1987. "Pagan Versions of the Rain Miracle of A.D. 172." *Historia* 36:83–95.

Garrett, Susan R. 1989. *The Demise of the Devil: Magic and the Demonic in Luke's Writings*. Minneapolis, Minn.: Fortress Press.

Gaster, Moses. 1971. *Studies and Texts in Folklore, Magic, Mediaeval Romance, Hebrew Apocrypha, and Samaritan Archaeology*. New York: Ktav.

Gersh, Stephen. 1978. *From Iamblichus to Eriugena: An Investigation of the Prehistory and Evolution of the Pseudo-Dionysian Tradition*. Leiden: Brill.

Gibbon, Edward. 1946. *The Decline and Fall of the Roman Empire*. New York: Heritage. First publication, 1776.

Ginzburg, Louis. 1905. "Yetsira." Pages 12:602–6 in *Jewish Encyclopedia*, ed. I. Singer. New York: Funk & Wagnalls.

Godwin, J. 1991. *The Mystery of the Seven Vowels in Theory and Practice*. Grand Rapids, Mich.: Phanes.

Gögler, Rolf. 1963. *Zur Theologie des biblischen Wortes bei Origenes*. Düsseldorf: Patmos.

Goshen-Gottstein, Alon. 1995. "Four Entered Paradise Revisited." *Harvard Theological Review* 88:69–133.

Graf, Fritz. 1997. *Magic in the Ancient World*. Cambridge, Mass.: Harvard University Press.

Green, William Scott. 1979. "Palestinian Holy Men: Charismatic Leadership and Rabbinic Tradition." Pages 619–47 in *Aufsteig und Niedergang der romischen Welt*, ed. W. Haase, 2.19.2. Berlin: De Gruyter.

Grozinger, Karl. 1987. "The Names of God and Their Celestial Powers." *Jerusalem Studies in Jewish Thought* 6:53–69.

Gruenbaum, Max. 1901. *Gesamelte Aufsatze zur Sprach- und Sagenkunde*. Berlin: Calvary.

Gruenwald, Ithamar. 1971. "A Preliminary Critical Edition of *Sefer Yezira*." *Israel Oriental Studies* 1:132–77.

———. 1973a. "Knowledge and Vision." *Israel Oriental Studies* 3:63–107.

———. 1973b. "Some Critical Notes on the First Part of *Sefer Yezira*." *Revue des Etudes Juives* 103:475–512.

———. 1980. *Apocalyptic and Merkavah Mysticism*. Leiden: Brill.

Guttman, Alexander. 1967. "The End of the Jewish Sacrificial Cult." *Hebrew Union College Annual* 38:137–48.

Hadot, Pierre. 1968. *Porphyre et Victorinus*. Paris: Etudes Augustiniennes.

Halleux, Robert. 1981. *Les alchimistes grecs*. Paris: Les Belles Lettres.

Halperin, David J. 1980. *The Merkabah in Rabbinic Literature*. New Haven, Conn.: American Oriental Society.

———. 1988. *The Faces of the Chariot: Early Jewish Responses to Ezekiel's Vision*. Tübingen: Mohr.

Hayward, Robert. 1974. "The Memra of YHWH and the Development of Its Use in Targum Neofiti I." *Journal of Jewish Studies* 25:412–18.

Heinemann, Joseph. 1977. *Prayer in the Talmud: Forms and Patterns*. Berlin. New York: De Gruyter.

Herrmann, Klaus. 1988. "Text und Fiktion: Zur Textüberlieferung des *Shi'ur Qoma*." *Frankfurter Jüdaischtische Beitrag* 16:89–142.

Himmelfarb, Martha. 1988. "Heavenly Ascent and the Relationship of the Apocalypses and the Hekhalot Literature." *Hebrew Union College Annual* 59:73–100.

———. 1993. *Ascent to Heaven in Jewish and Christian Apocalypses*. New York: Oxford University Press.

Hirschle, Maurus. 1979. *Sprachphilosophie und Namenmagie im Neuplatonismus: Mit e. Exkurs zu "Demokrit" B 142*. Meisenheim am Glan: Hain.

Holladay, Carl. 1983. *Fragments from Hellenistic Jewish Authors*, vol. 1: *The Historians*. Chico, Calif.: Scholars Press.

Hopkins, Arthur John. 1927. "Transmutations by Color: A Study of Earliest Alchemy." *Studien zur Geschichte der Chemie: Festgabe Edmund P. v. Lippman*, ed. J. Ruska. Vol. 9–14. Berlin: Springer.

———. 1934. *Alchemy, Child of Greek Philosophy*. New York: Columbia University Press.

Idel, Moshe. 1981. "The Concept of Torah in Hekhalot Literature and Its Metamorphoses in Kabbalah." *Jerusalem Studies in Jewish Thought* 1:323–84. Hebrew.

———. 1992. "Reification of Language in Jewish Mysticism." Pages 42–79 in *Mysticism and Language*, ed. S. Katz. New York: Oxford University Press.

Jackson, Howard M., ed. and trans. 1978. *Zosimos of Panoplis: On the Letter Omega*. Missoula, Mont.: Scholars Press.

Jakobson, Roman. 1972. "On Linguistic Aspects of Translation." Pages 155–75 in *Selected Writings 5*. The Hague: Mouton.

Janowitz, Naomi. 1989. *The Poetics of Ascent: Theories of Language in a Rabbinic Ascent Text*. Albany: State University of New York Press.

———. 1991. "Theories of Divine Names in Origen and Pseudo-Dionysius." *History of Religions* 31:359–72.

———. 2001. *Magic in the Roman World: Pagans, Jews, and Christians*. London: Routledge.

Jevons, F. B. 1908. "Graeco-Italian Magic." Pages 93–120 in *Anthropology and the Classics,* ed. R. R. Marett. New York: Oxford University Press.

Johnston, Sarah. 1990. *Hekate Soteira: A Study of Hekate's Role in the Chaldean Oracles and Related Literature.* Atlanta, Ga.: Scholars Press.

———. 1992. "Riders in the Sky: Cavalier Gods and Theurgic Salvation in the Second Century A.D." *Classical Philology* 87:303–21.

———. 1997. "Rising to the Occasion: Theurgic Ascent in Its Cultural Milieu." Pages 165–93 in *Envisioning Magic,* ed. Peter Schaefer and Hans Kippenberg. Leiden: Brill.

Jung, Carl Gustav. 1967. *Alchemical Studies.* Princeton: Princeton University Press.

Kasher, M. 1967. "Notes on sefer ha-razim." *Torah shelemah* 22:187–92.

Katz, Steven. 1978. "Language, Epistemology and Mysticism." Pages 22–74 in *Mysticism and Philosophical Analysis,* Studies in Philosophy and Religion 5. London: Sheldon Press.

———. 1988 Winter. "On Mysticism." *Journal of the American Academy of Religion* 56:751–57.

Kern-Ulmer, Brigitte. 1996. "The Depiction of Magic in Rabbinic Texts: The Rabbinic and the Greek Concept of Magic." *Journal for the Study of Judaism* 27(3):289–303.

Klein, Michael. 1972. *The Translation of Anthropomorphisms and Anthropopathisms in the Targumin.* N.p. (Israel).

Lange, Nicolas de. 1976. *Origen and the Jews: Studies in Jewish-Christian Relations in Third-Century Palestine.* Cambridge: Cambridge University Press.

Lauterbach, Jacob. 1936. "Tashlich." *Hebrew Union College Annual* 11:207–340.

———. 1939. "The Belief in the Power of the Word." *Hebrew Union College Annual* 14:287–302.

Lesses, Rebecca. 1998. *Ritual Practices to Gain Power.* Harrisburg, Pa.: Trinity Press.

Levenson, Jon. 1994. *Creation and the Persistence of Evil: The Jewish Drama of Divine Omnipotence.* Princeton: Princeton University Press.

Leveque, Pierre. 1959. *Aurea catena Homeri: Une étude sur l'allegorie grecque.* Annales litteraires de l'Université de Besançon. 2nd series, Civilisations de l'antiquité, 27. Paris: Les Belles Lettres.

Levias, C. 1905. "Gematria." Pages 589–92 in *Jewish Encyclopedia,* vol. 5, ed. Cyrus Adler. New York: Funk & Wagnalls.

Levine, Lee. 1975. *Caesarea Under Roman Rule.* Leiden: Brill.

Lewy, Hans. 1969. "Sentence Fragments and Nouns in Greek in Hekhalot Rabbati." Pages 59–65 in *Studies in Jewish Hellenism.* Jerusalem: Bialik Institute. Hebrew.

———. 1978. *Chaldaean Oracles and Theurgy: Mysticism, Magic, and Platonism in the Later Roman Empire.* Second edition. Paris: Etudes Augustiniennes.

Lieberman, Saul. 1939. *Sheki'in.* Jerusalem: Bamberger et Vahrman. Hebrew.

———. 1962. "Hellenism in Jewish Palestine: Studies in the Literary Transmission, Beliefs, and Manners of Palestine in the I Century B.C.E.–IV Century C.E." Second edition. New York: Jewish Theological Seminary of America.

———. 1965a. *Greek in Jewish Palestine: Studies in the Life and Manners of Jewish Palestine in the II–IV Centuries C.E.* Second edition. New York: P. Feldheim.

————. 1965b. "Mishnat Shir Hashirim." Pages 118–26 in *Jewish Gnosticism Merkabah Mysticism and Talmudic Tradition*, ed. G. Scholem. Second edition. New York: Jewish Theological Seminary of America.

————. 1974. "Some Notes on Adjurations in Israel." Pages 69–74 in *Texts and Studies*. New York: Ktav.

Lightstone, Jack N. 1984. *The Commerce of the Sacred: Mediation of the Divine Among Jews in the Graeco-Roman Diaspora*. Chico, Calif.: Scholars Press.

Lindsay, Jack. 1970. *The Origins of Alchemy in Graeco-Roman Egypt*. New York: Barnes & Noble.

Lippmann, E. o. v. 1919. *Entstehung und Ausbreitung der Alchemie*. Berlin: Springer.

Luck, Georg. 1989. "Theurgy and Forms of Worship in Neoplatonism." Pages 185–225 in *Religion, Science, and Magic: In Concert and in Conflict*, ed. Jacob Neusner, Ernest S. Frerichs, and Paul V. M. Flesher. New York: Oxford University Press.

Luibheid, Colm, and Paul Rorem. 1987. *Pseudo-Dionysius: The Complete Works*. New York: Paulist Press.

Luttikhuizen, Gerard P. 1985. *The Revelation of Elchasai: Investigations into the Evidence for a Mesopotamian Jewish Apocalypse of the Second Century and Its Reception by Judeo-Christian Propagandists*. Tübingen: Mohr.

Maier, Johann. 1968a. "Das Buch der Geheimnisse." *Judaica* 24:98–111.

————. 1968b. "Poetisch-liturgische Stucke aus dem 'Buch der Geheimnisse.'" *Judaica* 24:172–81.

————. 1973. "Serienbildung und 'numinoser' Eindruckseffeckt in den poetischen Stücken der Hekhalot Literatur." *Semitics* 3:36–66.

Majercik, Ruth. 1989. *The Chaldean Oracles: Text, Translation, and Commentary*. Leiden: Brill.

Mann, Jacob. 1931–35. *Text and Studies in Jewish History and Literature*. Cincinnati: Hebrew Union College Press.

Margalioth, Mordecai. 1966. *Sefer ha-razim*. Jerusalem: Keren Yehudah leb u-Mini Epshtein she-'al yad ha-Akademyah le-Mada'e ha-Yahadut be-Artsot ha-Berit. Hebrew.

Marmorstein, A. 1927. *The Old Rabbinic Doctrine of God*. New York: Oxford University Press.

Merchavya, Ch. 1966–67. "Review of Margalioth's *Sefer Ha-Razim*." *Kiryat Sefer* 42:188–92, 297–303. Hebrew.

————. 1971. "Sefer Ha-Razim." Pages 1594–95 in *Encyclopedia Judaica*, vol. 13. Jerusalem: Ktav.

Mertz, Elizabeth. 1996. "Recontextualization as Socialization: Text and Pragmatics in the Law School Classroom." Pages 229–49 in *Natural Histories of Discourse*, ed. Michael Silverstein and Greg Urban. Chicago: University of Chicago Press.

Mettinger, Tryggve N. D. 1982. *The Dethronement of Sabaoth: Studies in the Shem and Kabod Theologies*. Coniectanea Biblica, Old Testament Series 18. Lund: Gleerup.

Mitchell, Christopher Wright. 1987. *The Meaning of BRK "to bless" in the Old Testament*. Atlanta, Ga.: Scholars Press.

Mopsik, Charles. 1994. "La datation du Chi'our Qomah d'après néotestamentaire." *Revue des Sciences Religieuses* 68(2):131–44.

Morgan, Michael A. 1983. *Sepher ha-razim: The Book of the Mysteries.* Texts and translations, Pseudepigrapha series, 25.11. Chico, Calif.: Scholars Press.

Morray-Jones, C. R. A. 1992. "Transformational Mysticism in the Apocalyptic-Merkabah Tradition." *Journal of Jewish Studies* 43:1–31.

———. 1993. "Paradise Revisited (2 Corinthians 12:1–12): The Jewish Mystical Background of Paul's Apostolate, 1 and 2." *Harvard Theological Review* 86:177–217, 265–92.

———. Forthcoming. "The Body of the Glory: Si'ur Qomah and Transformational Mysticism in the Epistle of the Ephesians." Unpublished article.

Neale, J. M. 1976. *A History of the Holy Eastern Church.* New York: AMS Press.

Negev, A. 1973. "The Staircase-Tower in Nabatean Architechture." *Revue Biblique* 80:364–82.

Nemoy, Leon. 1930. "Al-Qirqisani's Account of the Jewish Sects and Christianity." *Hebrew Union College Annual* 7:317–97.

———. 1986. "Al-Qirqisani on the Occult Sciences." *Jewish Quarterly Review* 76:329–67.

Neusner, Jacob. 1966–70. *A History of the Jews in Babylonia.* Leiden: Brill.

———. 1969. "The Phenomenon of the Rabbi in Late Antiquity." *Numen* 19:1–20.

———. 1989. "Science and Magic, Miracle, and Magic in Formative Judaism: The System and the Difference." Pages 61–81 in *Religion, Science, and Magic: In Concert and in Conflict,* ed. Jacob Neusner, Ernest S. Frerichs, and Paul Virgil McCracken Flesher. New York: Oxford University Press.

Newsom, Carol. 1985. *Songs of the Sabbath Sacrifice: A Critical Edition.* Atlanta, Ga.: Scholars Press.

———. 1990a. "Sectually-Explicit" Literature from Qumran." Pages 167–87 in *The Hebrew Bible and Its Interpreters,* ed. William Henry Propp, Baruch Halpern, and David Noel Freedman. Winona Lake, Ind.: Eisenbrauns.

———. 1990b. "He Has Established Himself Priests": Human and Angelic Priesthood in the Qumran Shabbath *Shirot.*" Pages 101–20 in *Archaeology and History in the Dead Sea Scrolls,* ed. Lawrence Schiffman. Sheffield: Sheffield Academic Press.

Niggemeyer, J. H. 1975. *Beschworungsformeln aus dem "Buch der Gehemnisse."* Hildersheim: Georg Olms Verlag.

Nilsson, Martin. 1948. *Greek Piety.* Oxford: Clarendon.

———. 1963. "The High God and the Mediator." *Harvard Theological Review* 56:101–20.

Nock, Arthur Darby, ed. and trans. 1966. *Sallustius: Concerning the Gods and the Universe.* Hildesheim: Georg Olms.

Parmentier, Richard. 1985. "Semiotic Mediation: Ancestral Genealogy and Final Interpretant." Pages 359–85 in Richard Parmentier and Elizabeth Mertz eds., *Semiotic Mediation.* Orlando, Fla.: Academic Press.

———. 1994. *Signs in Society: Studies in Semiotic Anthropology.* Bloomington: Indiana University Press.

Patai, Raphael. 1994. *The Jewish Alchemists: A History and Source Book*. Princeton: Princeton University Press.

Pearson, Birger. 1981. *Nag Hammadi Codices IX and X*. Leiden: Brill.

———. 1984. "Gnosticism as Platonism, with Special Reference to Marsanes (NCH 10.1)." *Harvard Theological Review* 77:55–72.

Peirce, Charles. 1940. *The Philosophical Writings of Charles Peirce*. New York: Dover.

Penner, Hans. 1983. "The Mystical Illusion." Pages 89–116 in *Mysticism and Religious Traditions*, ed. S. Katz. New York: Oxford University Press.

Pfister, R. 1935. *Teinture et Alchimie dans l'orient hellenistique*. Seminarium Kondakovianum. Praha: Institut Kondakov.

Phillips, C. R. 1986. "The Sociology of Religious Knowledge in the Roman Empire to A.D. 284." Pages 2677–773 in *Aufsteig und Niedergang der römischen Welt, vol. 2: Principat*, ed. W. Hasse. Berlin: De Gruyter.

Pines, Shlomo. 1989. "Points of Similarity Between the Exposition of the Doctrine of the Sefirot in the Sefer Yezira and a Text of the Pseudo-Clementine Homilies: The Implications of This Resemblance." Pages 63–142 in *Israel Academy of Sciences and Humanities Proceedings*, vol. 7.

Places, Edouard des, ed. and trans. 1971. *Oracles Chaldaïques*. Paris: Les Belles Lettres.

———. 1983. "Notes sur quelques oracles chaldaïques." Pages 319–30 in *Mélanges Edouard Delebecque*. Aix-en-Provence: Université de Provence.

———. 1984. "Les Oracles chaldaïques." Pages 2299–335 in *Aufsteig und Niedergang der römischen Welt*, vol. 2.17.4, ed. W. Haase. Berlin: De Gruyter.

Plessner, M. 1976. "Zosimus." Pages 631–32 in *Dictionary of Scientific Biography*, vol. 14, ed. C. Gillispie. New York: Charles Scribner's Sons.

Praechter, Karl. 1934. "Theodoros." Pages 2–10 in *Paulys Realencyclopädie der Classischen Altertumswissenschaft*, 2nd series, vol. 10, 1833–38. Stuttgart: Alfred Druckenmüller Verlag.

Price, Simon. 1984. "Gods and Emperors: The Greek Language of the Roman Imperial Cult." *Journal of Hellenic Studies* 104:79–95.

———. 1987. "From Noble Funeral to Divine Cult: The Consecration of Roman Emperors." Pages 56–105 in *Ritual of Royalty: Power and Ceremonial in Traditional Societies*, ed. David Cannadine and Simon Price. Cambridge: Cambridge University Press.

Proudfoot, Wayne. 1985. *Religious Experience*. Berkeley and Los Angeles: University of California Press.

Rappaport, Roy. 1980. "Concluding Comments on Ritual and Reflexivity." *Semiotica* 30:181–93.

Rappe, Sara. 1995. "Metaphor in Plotinus' *Enneads* 5.8.9." *Ancient Philosophy* 15:155–72.

Reif, Stefan C. 1993. *Judaism and Hebrew Prayer: New Perspectives on Jewish Liturgical History*. Cambridge: Cambridge University Press.

Riess, Ernst. 1893. "Alchemie." Pages 1338–55 in *Paulys Realencyclopädie der Classischen Altertumswissenschaft*, vol. 1, ed. Georg. Wissowa. Stuttgart: Alfred Druckenmüller Verlag.

Rist, John M. 1967. *Plotinus: The Road to Reality.* Cambridge: Cambridge University Press.

Roberts, A., and J. Donaldson, eds. 1979. *The Apostolic Fathers with Justin Martyr and Irenaeus,* vol. 1 of *The Ante-Nicene Christian Fathers, Translations of the Writings of the Fathers Down to a.d. 325.* Grand Rapids, Mich.: Eerdmans.

Rudolph, Kurt. 1983. *Gnosis: The Nature and History of an Ancient Religion.* Edinburgh: T. & T. Clark.

Ruelle, C. E. 1889. "Le chant des sept voyelles grecques d'aprés Démétrius et les papyrus de Leyde." *Revue des Etudes Grecques* 2:38–44.

Saffrey, H. D. 1981. "Les Néoplatoniciens et les Oracles Chaldaïques." *Revue des Etudes Augustiniennes* 26:209–25.

———. 1982. "New Objective Links Between the Pseudo-Dionysius and Proclus." Pages 64–74 in *Neoplatonism and Christian Thought,* ed. D. O'Meara. Albany: State University of New York Press.

Sathas, C. 1875. "Sur les commentaires byzantine." *Annuaire de l'Association des Etudes Grecques* 9:187–222.

Schäfer, Peter. 1987. *übersetzungen der Hekhalot-Literatur.* Tübingen: Mohr.

———. 1988a. "The Problem of the Redactional Identity of Hekhalot Rabbati." Pages 63–74 in *Hekhalot-Studien.* Tübingen: Mohr. German.

———. 1988b. "Shiur Qoma: Rezensionen und Urtext." Pages 75–83 in *Hekhalot- Studien.* Tübingen: Mohr.

———. 1990. "Jewish Magic Literature in Late Antiquity and Early Modern Ages." *Journal of Jewish Studies* 41(1):75–91.

———. 1992. *The Hidden and Manifest God: Some Major Themes in Early Jewish Mysticism.* Albany: State University of New York Press.

———. 1996. "Jewish Liturgy and Magic." Pages 1:531–55 in *Geschichte—Tradition— Reflexion.* Tübingen: Mohr.

Schäfer, Peter, Margarete Schlüter, and Hans-Georg von Mutius. 1981. *Synopse zur Hekhalot-Literatur.* Tübingen: Mohr.

Schiffman, Lawrence. 1982. "Merkavah Speculation at Qumran: The 4Q Sereckh Shirot 'Olat ha-Shabbat." Pages 15–47 of *Mystics, Philosophers, and Politicians,* ed. J. Reinhartz. Durham, N.C.: Duke University Press.

Schlüter, Margarete. 1985. "Untersuchungen zur Form und Funktion der *Berakha* in der *Hekhalot-*Literatur." *Frankfurter Judaistische Beitrage* 13:83–146.

Scholem, Gershom. 1954. *Major Trends in Jewish Mysticism.* Third edition. New York: Schocken Books.

———. 1965a. *Jewish Gnosticism, Merkabah Mysticism, and Talmudic Tradition.* New York: Jewish Theological Seminary of America.

———. 1965b. *On the Kabbalah and Its Symbolism.* New York: Schocken Books.

———. 1972a. "The Name of God and the Linguistic Theory of the Kabbalah." *Diogenes* 79/80:59–80, 164–94.

———. 1972b. "Gematria." Pages 369–74 in *Encyclopedia Judaica,* vol. 7. Jerusalem: Ktav.

———. 1991. *On the Mystical Shape of the Godhead: Basic Concepts in the Kabbalah.* New York: Schocken.

Segal, Alan. 1980. "Heavenly Ascent in Hellenistic Judaism, Early Christianity, and Their Environment." Pages 1333–94 in *Aufsteig und Niedergang der römischen Welt, II, Principat*, ed. W. Hasse, vol. 23. Berlin: De Gruyter.

———. 1981. "Hellenistic Magic: Some Questions of Definition." Pages 349–75 in *Studies in Gnosticism and Hellenistic Religion Presented to Gilles Quispel*, ed. R. van den Broek and M. J. Vermasseren. Leiden: Brill.

Shaw, Gregory. 1985. "Theurgy: Rituals of Unification in the Neoplatonism of Iamblichus." *Traditio* 41:1–28.

———. 1995. *Theurgy and the Soul: The Neoplatonism of Iamblichus*. University Park, Pa: The Pennsylvania State University Press.

Sheldon-Williams, I. P. 1972. "Henads and Angels: Proclus and the Ps. Dionysius." *Studia Patristica* 11:65–71.

Sheriff, John K. 1989. *The Fate of Meaning: Charles Peirce, Structuralism, and Literature*. Princeton: Princeton University Press.

Silverstein, Michael. 1976. "Shifters: Linguistic Categories and Cultural Descriptions." Pages 11–55 in *Meaning in Anthropology*, ed. K. Basso and H. Selby. Albuquerque: University of New Mexico.

———. 1978. "Language Structure and Linguistic Ideology." Pages 193–247 in *The Elements*, ed. P. Clyne, W. Hanks, and C. Hofhaur. Chicago: Chicago Linguistic Society.

———. 1981. "Metaforces of Power in Traditional Oratory." Unpublished lecture.

———. 1993. "Metapragmatic Discourse and Metapragmatic Function." Pages 33–58 in *Reflexive Language: Reported Speech and Metapragmatics*, ed. J. Lucy. Cambridge: Cambridge University Press.

Simon, Marcel. 1986. *Verus Israel: A Study of the Relations Between Christians and Jews in the Roman Empire (135–425)*. New York: Oxford University Press.

Smith, Andrew. 1974. *Porphyry's Place in the Neoplatonic Tradition: A Study in Post-Plotinian Neoplatonism*. The Hague: M. Nijhoff.

Smith, Huston. 1990. "Is There Perennial Philosophy?" *Journal of the American Academy of Religion* 55:553–66.

Smith, Jonathan Z. 1974. "Hellenistic Religions." Pages 749–51 in *Encyclopedia Britannica*, vol. 8. Chicago.

———. 1978. *Map Is Not Territory: Studies in the History of Religions*. Studies in Judaism in Late Antiquity 23. Leiden: Brill.

———. 1982. *Imagining Religion: From Babylon to Jonestown*. Chicago Studies in the History of Judaism. Chicago: University of Chicago Press.

Smith, Morton. 1963. "Observations on Hekhalot Rabbati." Pages 142–60 in *Biblical and Other Studies*, ed. A. Altmann. Cambridge, Mass.: Harvard University Press.

———. 1965. "The Ascent of Simon Magus in Acts 8." Pages 735–49 in *Harry Austryn Wolfson Jubilee Volume on the Occasion of His Seventy-Fifth Birthday, English Section*, ed. Harry Austryn Wolfson. Jerusalem: American Academy for Jewish Research.

———. 1973. *Clement of Alexandria and a Secret Gospel of Mark*. Cambridge, Mass.: Harvard University Press.

———. 1978. *Jesus the Magician*. New York: Harper & Row.

———. 1979. "Relations Between Magical Papyri and Magical Gems." *Papyrologica Brux-ellensia* 18:129–36.

———. 1981. "Ascent to the Heavens and the Beginning of Christianity." *Eranos Jahrbuch* 50:403–29.

———. 1982. "Helios in Palestine." *Erets-Yisra'el* 16:199–214.

———. 1986. "Salvation in the Gospels, Paul, and the Magical Papyri." *Helios* 13:63–74.

———. 1990. "Ascent to the Heavens and Deification in 4MQa." Pages 181–88 in *Archaeology and History in the Dead Sea Scrolls*, ed. Lawrence Schiffman. Sheffield: Sheffield Academic Press.

Sperber, Daniel. 1966. "On Sealing the Abyss." *Journal of Semitic Studies* 11:168–74.

Stambursky, Samuel. 1976. "The Source and Reality of the Term 'Gematria,'" *Tarbits* 45:268–71.

Stern, Menachem. 1974–84. *Greek and Latin Authors on Jews and Judaism*. Jerusalem: Israel Academy of Sciences and Humanities.

Swartz, Michael D. 1990. "Scribal Magic and Its Rhetoric: Formal Patterns in Medieval Hebrew and Aramaic Incantation Texts from the Cairo-Genizah." *Harvard Theological Review* 83:163–80.

———. 1996. *Scholastic Magic: Ritual and Revelation in Early Jewish Mysticism*. Princeton: Princeton University Press.

Tabor, James. 1986. *Things Unutterable: Paul's Ascent to Paradise in Its Greco-Roman, Judaic, and Early Christian Contexts*. Lanham, Md.: University Press of America.

Talmon, S. 1978. "The Emergence of Institutionalized Prayer in Judaism in the Light of the Qumran Literature." Pages 265–84 in *Qumran: Sa piété, sa théologie, et son milieu*, ed. M. Delcor. Paris: Leuven.

Tambiah, Stanley J. 1968. "The Magical Power of Words." *Man* 3:175–208.

———. 1979. "A Performative Approach to Ritual." *Proceedings of the British Academy* 113–69.

———. 1985. *Culture, Thought, and Social Action: An Anthropological Perspective*. Cambridge, Mass.: Harvard University Press.

———. 1990. *Magic, Science, Religion, and the Scope of Rationality*. Cambridge: Cambridge University Press.

Taylor, F. Sherwood. 1930. "A Survey of Greek Alchemy." *Journal of Hellenistic Studies* 50:109–39.

———. 1937. "The Origins of Greek Alchemy." *Ambix* 1:1–37.

———. 1949. *The Alchemists, Founders of Modern Chemistry*. New York: H. Schuman.

Thee, Francis C. R. 1984. *Julius Africanus and the Early Christian View of Magic*. Tübingen: Mohr.

Trouillard, Jean. 1975. "L'activité onomatique selon Proclos." Pages 239–51 in *De Jamblique à Proclus*. Geneva: Vandoeuvres.

Vaux, R. de 1970. "The Revelation of the Divine Name YHWH." Pages 40–75 in *Proclamation and Presence: Old Testament Essays in Honor of G. H. Davies*, ed. J. I. Durham and J. R. Porter. Richmond, Va.: John Knox.

Versnel, H. S. 1991. "Magic and Religion—Some Reflections on the Relationship." *Numen* 38:177–97.

Waszink, J. H. 1950. "Biothanati." Pages 391–94 in *Reallexikon fur Antike und Christentum,* vol. 2, ed. Theodor Klauser. Stuttgart: Hiersemann.

Weltin, E. G. 1960. "The Concept of *Ex-Opere-Operato* Efficacy in the Fathers as Evidence of Magic in Early Christianity." *Greek, Roman, and Byzantine Studies* 3:74–100.

Wenschkewitz, H. 1932. "Die Spritiualisierung der Kultusbegriffe: Tempel, Priester und Opfer im NeuenTestament." *Angelos* 4:71–230.

Wernberg-Moller, P. 1962. "An Inquiry into the Validity of the Text-Critical Argument for an Early Dating of the Recently Discovered Palestinian Targum." *Vetus Testamentum* 12:312–30.

Wolfson, Elliot. 1987. "Circumcision and the Divine Name: A Study in the Transmission of Esoteric Doctrine." *Jewish Quarterly Review* 78:77–112.

————. 1994. *Through a Speculum That Shines: Vision and Imagination in Medieval Jewish Mysticism.* Princeton: Princeton University Press.

Wutz, Franz. 1914. *Onomastica Sacra: Untersuchungen zum Liber Interpretationis Nominum Hebraicorum des Hieronymus.* Texte und Untersuchungen zur Geschichte der altchristlichen literatur, 41.1. Leipzig: J. C. Hinrich.

Yadin, Yigael. 1962. *The Scroll of the War of the Sons of Light Against the Sons of Darkness.* London: Oxford University Press.

York, Anthony. 1974. "The Dating of Targumic Literature." *Journal for the Study of Judaism* 5:49–62.

Zaehner, R. C. 1960. *Hindu and Muslim Mysticism.* London: University of London, Athlone Press.

Primary Source Index

* See Bibliography, Primary Sources for edition cited

General Index

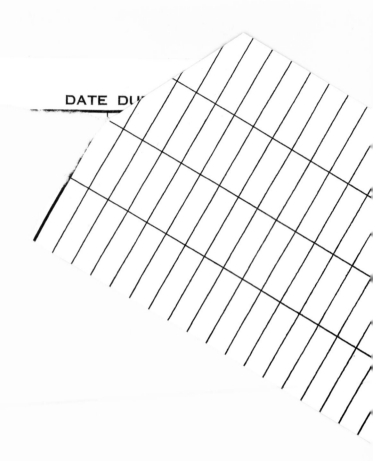

DATE DU